Thematic Unit
World War I

Written by Sarah K. Clark

Teacher Created Materials, Inc.
P.O. Box 1040
Huntington Beach, CA 92647
©1997 Teacher Created Materials, Inc.
Made in U.S.A.

ISBN 1-55734-598-8

Edited by
Stephanie Buehler, M.P.W., M.A.

Illustrated by
Howard Chaney

Cover Art by
Jose Tapia

Table of Contents

Introduction

World War I is a comprehensive whole language, thematic unit. Its 80 reproducible pages are filled with a wide variety of lesson ideas designed for use with intermediate and junior high school students. At its core are two high-quality reading selections, *World War I* and *After the Dancing Days*.

Activities for each selection set the stage for reading, encourage the enjoyment of the book, and extend the concepts. Activities are also provided that integrate the curriculum areas of language arts (including writing and research skills), math, science, social studies, art, music, and life skills. Many of the activities are conducive to the use of cooperative learning groups.

Unit Management tools include time-saving suggestions such as patterns for bulletin boards and learning centers. The activities allow students to synthesize their knowledge and make the events of World War I come to life.

This thematic unit includes:

❑ **Literature selections:** two books with related lessons that cross the curriculum

❑ **Planning guides:** suggestions for sequencing lessons of the unit

❑ **Poetry and drama:** suggested selections and lessons that enable students to write, perform, and publish their own works

❑ **Writing ideas:** daily writing suggestions and activities that cross the curriculum, including student-created books

❑ **Bulletin boards:** suggestions and plans for content related and interactive bulletin boards

❑ **Home/school connections:** for extending the unit to the student's home and family

❑ **Curriculum connections:** ties between language arts, math, science, social studies, art, music, and life skills

❑ **Group projects:** fostering cooperative learning

❑ **Culminating activities:** requiring students to synthesize their learning and produce products that can be shared with others

❑ **Bibliography:** additional literature and nonfiction books relating to the theme

---

To keep this valuable resource intact so that it can be used year after year, you may wish to punch holes in the pages and store them in a three-ring binder.

Introduction *(cont.)*

Why Whole Language?

A whole language approach involves children in using all modes of communication: reading, writing, listening, speaking, observing, illustrating, experiencing, and doing. Communication skills are interconnected and integrated into lessons that emphasize the whole of language rather than isolating its parts. The lessons revolve around selected literature. Reading is not taught as a separate subject from writing and spelling. A child reads, writes, speaks, listens, and thinks in response to a literature experience introduced by the teacher. In this way, language skills grow naturally, stimulated by involvement and interest in the topic at hand.

Why Thematic Planning?

One very useful tool for implementing an integrated whole language program is thematic planning. By choosing a theme with correlating literature selections for a unit of study, a teacher can plan activities throughout the day that lead to a cohesive, in-depth study of the topic. Students will be practicing and applying their skills in meaningful contexts. Consequently, they will tend to learn and retain more. Both teachers and students will be freed from a day that is broken into unrelated segments of isolated drill and practice.

Why Cooperative Learning?

Besides academic skills and content, students need to learn social skills. No longer can this area of development be taken for granted. Students must learn to work cooperatively in groups in order to function well in modern society. Group activities should be a regular part of school life and teachers should consciously include social objectives as well as academic objectives in their planning. The teacher should clarify and monitor the qualities of good group interaction, just as he or she clarifies and monitors the academic goals of the project.

World War I

Summary

World War I is a nonfiction book that captures the reader's attention with realistic, play-by-play descriptions of the events of World War I. Author Peter Bosco writes detailed descriptions of such events as the Battle of Belleau Wood, the Argonne, and the sinking of the Lusitania.

The book also includes maps, illustrations, charts, strategies of military and political leaders, personal quotes from people directly involved with the war, and touching tributes to the soldiers who fought.

Each of the lessons suggested below may take from one to several days to complete.

Sample Plan

Lesson 1
- ❏ Introduce *World War I* (see "Overview of Activities," pages 6–10).
- ❏ Assemble "WWI Notebooks" and discuss "World War I Journal" (page 11).
- ❏ Assemble bulletin boards and World War I time line (page 73).
- ❏ Assign reading pages for each day and have students sign "Agreement Form" (page 13).
- ❏ Read Chapters 1–4 of *World War I*. Begin chapter activities (pages 14–17).
- ❏ Do the "Times Are Changing" lesson (page 12).
- ❏ Perform "Trouble in the Cafeteria" skit (page 61–64).

Lesson 2
- ❏ Complete the following:
  "Causes of the Great War" (page 21).
  "Map of a Divided Europe" (page 20).
  "The Sinking of the *Lusitania*" (page 22).
- ❏ Read Chapters 5–8 in *World War I*.
- ❏ Continue chapter activities (pages 14–17).

Lesson 3
- ❏ Read Chapters 9–12 in *World War I*.
- ❏ Continue chapter activities (pages 14–17).
- ❏ Complete the following:
  "War Bond Poster" (page 65).
  "Songs of World War I" (page 23).

Lesson 4
- ❏ Read Chapters 13–16 in *World War I*.
- ❏ Continue chapter activities (pages 14–17).
- ❏ Complete the following:
  "Mention My Invention" (page 24)
  "Alliances" (page 60)
  "WWI Poetry" (page 49)
  "Famous Faces of WWI" (page 57).

Lesson 5
- ❏ Read Chapters 17–19 in *World War I*.
- ❏ Continue chapter activities (pages 14–17).
- ❏ Complete the following:
- ❏ "Cooking on the Western Front" (page 67)
- ❏ "The Deadly Virus" (page 55)
- ❏ "Fact or Opinion?" (page 27)
- ❏ "Finish the Story" (page 50)
- ❏ "Wars Are Hard to Predict" (page 53)

Lesson 6
- ❏ Read Chapters 20–21 in *World War I*.
- ❏ Continue chapter activities (pages 14–17).
- ❏ Complete the following:
  "Graphing the Great War" (page 25)
  "Causes and Effects of WWI" (page 26)
  "Newsworthy Notes" (page 51)
  "Now and Then" (page 59)
  "WWI Quiz Game" (page 68–69)
  "WWI Projects" (pages 71–72)

Overview of Activities

Setting the Stage

1. Assemble the "World War I: A Time of Change" bulletin board (page 73). Then assemble the "True or False" learning center (page 74) and the "Did You Know?" bulletin board (page 75).

2. Assemble student World War I notebooks (page 11). Each student needs a three-ring binder divided into two sections. The first section should be labeled "World War I." This is where students will collect handouts and assignments they have completed. Be sure to make copies of the "Important Dates of World War I" (page 18) and *World War I* Vocabulary" (page 19) for students to store in their binders throughout the unit. Do not let them discard any pages or activities from the WWI unit. They will need these pages to work on future WWI assignments. The second section should be labeled "WWI Journal."

3. Construct a time line to display in your classroom using clothesline, yarn, or adding machine tape. This time line is where students and the teacher will be able to add events of World War I as they are studied.

4. Create a "KWL" chart. On a large piece of butcher paper, write the words "Know," "Want to Know," and "Learned" horizontally across the top. Have your students turn to the first page in their journals and copy these words across the top. Ask the students to write down all the things they know about World War I under the word "Know" and all the things they want to know under the "Want to Know" column. Then gather together in a group and have students share all the things they know and want to know about World War I. Record these answers on the butcher paper. Display this in a prominent place in the classroom so that as learning occurs it can be recorded under the "Learned" column. When you are putting closure to the end of the unit, pull this chart out to help students clarify and cement their learning.

Know	Want to Know	Learned

5. Make preparations to teach the "Times Are Changing" lesson on page 12. Once the lesson is completed, discuss briefly with students the changes that began to take place in the world and in the United States as a result of World War I. Introduce the book *America at War: World War I* by Peter Bosco. Explain to students that you will be using this book to gain an understanding of World War I and the changes it brought. Allow students a chance to browse through the book and to share their thoughts as they glance at the illustrations. Is there something that can be added to your KWL chart? (See #4 above.)

Overview of Activities *(cont.)*

Setting the Stage *(cont.)*

6. Assign pages for reading. (See page 13 for "Student Agreement" form.) *World War I* comes in hardback only. For financial reasons, you may wish to have students share. You may use a variety of techniques such as whole class reading, one student or teacher reading to everyone, setting times for students to read individually, and buddy reading. You will have to be sensitive to the amount of reading required as homework if two students are sharing a book.

7. At the end of the first day of class on World War I, send home the parent letter on page 76. Prepare a World War I Research Center to keep fiction and nonfiction books, maps, encyclopedias, pictures, and items brought by students from home to share, as well as other materials available for students to use with World War I projects and activities during the unit.

Day	Reading Assignment	Discussion Questions	Activities	Journal Questions
Day One	Chapters 1–4			
Day Two	Chapters 5–8			
Day Three	Chapters 9–12			
Day Four	Chapters 13–16			
Day Five	Chapters 17–19			
Day Six	Chapter 20–21			

8. As a homework assignment at the beginning of the World War I unit, ask students to bring in newspaper articles about a local, state, country, or world conflict. Share the articles in small groups, allowing students to summarize the main ideas. Then, in the same groups, have students record on a sheet of paper what the newspaper articles had in common. Discuss as a class the continuous themes that recur in conflicts. Save group papers to be used in a future activity. (See "Dilemma—A Time for Making Decisions" on page 66).

Enjoying the Book

1. Review the skit, "Trouble in the Cafeteria," on pages 61–64. Students selected to play characters will need to meet at lunch or other times outside of class to prepare this skit for the rest of the class to watch. Have each member memorize his or her part and come dressed accordingly. Early in the unit, present this skit to the class. Each character represents a country and its role in World War I. Immediately after the skit, discuss each of the characters involved. (See "Map of a Divided Europe" on page 20.) Provide the students with the names of each country, briefly discussing its role and the side it was on during World War I.

2. Read and discuss "Causes and Effects of World War I" using page 26. There are four main causes: nationalism, imperialism, militarism, and the system of alliances. Students will need plenty of time to discuss and clarify the meaning of these words and concepts.

3. Locate each of the main countries involved in World War I on the "Map of a Divided Europe" (page 20). Color code the map into three groups of countries: the Central Powers, the Allies, and the countries that remained neutral.

Overview of Activities *(cont.)*

Enjoying the Book *(cont.)*

4. Show the video, "Secrets of the Unknown: The *Lusitania*" (see the Bibliography, pages 77–78, or use Chapter One of *World War I* if you cannot obtain the video). Copy "The Sinking of the *Lusitania*" (page 22) for students to preview and complete during the video. As an extension, discuss and analyze the theories brought up in the video. Take a class vote to decide what students think really happened to the *Lusitania*.

5. It took a true campaign to elicit the support of the American public for U.S. involvement in WWI. Posters advertised war bonds that people could purchase to help fund the war effort. Have students design and create their own war bond posters using page 65. Have a contest to see which poster is the best.

6. Much information can be gathered from songs that were written during the time period of WWI. Research local music stores to see if any of the songs listed on page 23 are available to play for the students in class. You may also find that parents or grandparents may be able to get copies of these songs to share with the class. See page 23 also for a student activity on the songs of WWI.

7. The need for faster, quicker, and more powerful war weapons brought about numerous inventions during this time period. As a class, research the U-boats, the machine gun, the tanks, and the airplane. How did these inventions change the war? Complete the "Mention My Invention" activity on page 24. Have students design and create their own inventions that would solve a problem. Hold an invention convention to display and model new ideas and ways of doing things.

8. The menu for the soldiers during WWI was not of the best quality. Sometimes the food was rotten as well. French troops called their rations "monkey meat" because it consisted of corned beef that had spoiled before being canned. Other rations were on the more pleasant side. Set up a kitchen in your classroom and try out some of the recipes from "Cooking on the Western Front" (page 67).

9. Sharpen students' graphing skills by graphing WWI information and selecting the appropriate graph. Copy "Graphing the Great War" (page 25) for each student.

10. Discuss and evaluate the causes and effects of World War I. Then provide each student with a copy of page 21 to complete individually and discuss in small groups.

11. Many times it is unclear if what we learn about history is fact or opinion. Copy and use the "Fact or Opinion" handout on page 27. As an extension of this activity, have students write their own statements about World War I and have the class guess whether these are facts or opinions.

Overview of Activities *(cont.)*

Enjoying the Book *(cont.)*

12. Provide each student with a copy of "Newsworthy Notes" on page 51. Have each student select an event from WWI. Ask students to imagine they are newspaper reporters and have just received a tip on the event they have selected. Student reporters can conduct research and write about the event. Have reporters write a newspaper article about their event and write it as though it happened recently. As an extension, put together a WWI newspaper. Hold a contest to determine the name of the newspaper. Invite artistically talented students to design pictures to accompany newspaper stories or to design political cartoons. Other students may write an editorial page on their thoughts of WWI.

13. Many of the doughboys died before returning home from WWI because of the epidemic that spread throughout the camps. Copy "The Deadly Virus" for each student to complete (page 55). Discuss disease prevention. You may also keep track of and chart who in class comes down with an illness and when it occurs. See if you can discover a pattern as to the type of sickness and the number of people infected as an introduction to epidemiology.

14. The concept of forming alliances was prevalent in World War I. Have students take a personal look at the alliances they have formed. Use "Alliances" to help with this discussion (page 60).

Extending the Book

1. Using your local library or the Internet, locate a school in France, Germany, or other country involved with World War I. Ask a classroom teacher there if his or her class would be willing to be pen pals. Write letters to pen pals asking them their opinions on WWI. Find out what they are taught about it in their schools.

2. Expose students to "word cinquain" poetry. This activity allows students to describe the conditions and realities of war. Find samples of word cinquains to share with the students. Be sure to discuss how the word cinquain is put together. Work as a class to complete a few before students write their own World War I cinquains. Use "World War I Poetry" (page 49) to help with this lesson.

3. Make copies of "Finish the Story" (page 50) for each student. Have students select a story opener. Students make the decision posed in the opener and write a short story about their imaginary war experience. Share these stories as a class. Bind them together to make a class book on fiction stories about World War I. You may also post these stories on the "World War I: The War to End All Wars" bulletin board (page 73) for others to see and read.

Overview of Activities *(cont.)*

Extending the Book *(cont.)*

4. Students will become more familiar with some of the people involved with World War I after they complete "Famous Faces of World War I" (page 57). First, have students attempt to fill out this page without any outside help. Then, allow students to use their books and other resources necessary to finish the page.

5. Review problem-solving skills using the student page, "Wars are Hard to Predict" (page 53). Students may work individually or with a partner. Have students check each others' work and then have the answer key available for students to check their own work when they are finished.

6. As individuals or in pairs, have the students compare and contrast how things were during World War I to how they are now using the "Now and Then" activity (page 59). Are some things similar? What things have changed?

7. As a culminating activity, allow students to choose a WWI project that they would like to complete. Projects and directions are found on pages 71 and 72. Together decide upon a time line to have these projects completed and ready to present. Have students fill out and sign the "WWI Project Contract" (page 72). Decide ahead as a class how the students would like to present these projects. In pairs? In front of the class? Presented to another class? Presented to the parents? In a display?

8. To help review and cement student learning, play the "WWI Quiz Game" (pages 68 and 69).

9. For a change of pace, give a test on World War I in a different way. Ask students to brainstorm as a class questions that could appear on a World War I test. After all questions have been recorded, select as a class the top eleven questions they would like to see on the test. Students then know the questions and prepare for the test. On the day of the test, select ten of the questions for students to answer. Students will feel more ownership for the test and hopefully the responsibility to study for it. As an extension, play the game Tic–Tac–Go (page 70) to help students study for the test.

World War I Journal

Throughout this unit, students will be asked to write down their thoughts, ideas, guesses, feelings, opinions and suggestions. Asking students to write these down is crucial in helping them make connections between their own lives and the history which they are studying.

These journal entries should flow naturally from the lessons taught or from class discussions. The entries are most successful when the students see them as an opportunity to explore and create ideas. Try to create a positive feeling for writing in the journals. Vary the time in the lesson that students write in their journals to keep the task from becoming mundane; journal entries can be written at the beginning, during, and at the end of a lesson.

Suggestions:

Each student will need a three-ring binder divided into two sections. The first section is for students to keep World War I pages and handouts, and the second section is for students to keep the journal entries.

Journal entries should not be written as though another person is feeling or thinking these things unless the students are specifically asked to assume the role of someone else in answering a question.

Be sure to have students write the date at the beginning of each journal entry. This journal will become a record of the journey that students will take during this unit on World War I. Each student's opinion may change from the beginning of the unit to the end. Much learning takes place when ideas are shared.

Extension:

Create a parent/student journal. The same questions you ask students can be asked of the parents or grandparents. Students will learn from the opinions and ideas of those who either lived through World War I or had family experiences associated with World War I. What an opportunity to share, in an informal setting, feelings, emotions, and ideas across the generations!

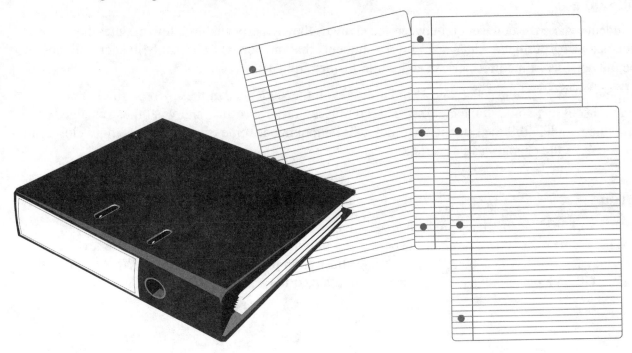

Times Are Changing

Lesson Outcome: The student will be able to describe feelings associated with change and learn of changes that took place during WWI.

Time Allotment: 45 minutes

Materials:

- Two pieces of butcher paper
- Marker
- Student Journals

Preparation: For this lesson, the students will need to experience an obvious change. Some suggestions of how to change could be to turn their chairs upside down, change your name (wear a name tag), speak a different language, rearrange desks, change the order in which you teach your subjects, call the students by their last names, turn the lights out, etc. Choose at least three of these ways to change the environment in the classroom, the idea being to change one physical item, one aural item, and one visual item. As a hint, write the word *change* on the board in large letters. It is best to make changes just before students are due to come into the classroom.

Activity

When students come into the classroom, begin teaching a "pretend" lesson (spelling, math, etc.) as usual, acting as though nothing is different. After a certain amount of time has passed and the feeling of change is prevalent, ask the students to write down those feelings in their journals.

When they have finished writing, begin recording on the butcher paper some of the feelings, thoughts, and ideas that the students had about the changes they experienced. Record all of the ideas, whether they are positive or not.

Discussion

Help students make the connection between the changes they experienced in a few minutes to the changes occurring during World War I. Inform students that the new topic of study in social studies will be the period of time in American and world history from 1914–1918.

Explain the "WWI Time Line" (page 18). Discuss with the students that they will be finding out about and discussing some of the changes that took place during this time and what these changes meant to the people. Tell the students that they will be looking at some of these events more closely in order to analyze the changes and experiences.

Extension

As a homework assignment, have students make their own personal time line of their lives so far. Perhaps they have experienced a major event such as a divorce in their family, or a smaller event, such as when they learned to ride a bike. Draw a small illustration to go with each event. What changes do they think will take place in the next five years? In the next ten?

Student Agreement Form

I,_____, agree to read *World War I,* written by Peter Bosco. This book has a total of 119 pages. Each day I need to answer discussion questions, do activities, and answer journal entries. I will use the following chart to help me keep track of assignments.

Day	Reading Assignment	Discussion Questions	Activities	Journal Questions
Day One	Chapters 1–4			
Day Two	Chapters 5–8			
Day Three	Chapters 9–12			
Day Four	Chapters 13–16			
Day Five	Chapters 17–19			
Day Six	Chapter 20–21			

World War I: Chapter Activities

Chapters 1–4

Activities

Before starting the book *World War I*, have student volunteers perform the skit, "Trouble in the Cafeteria" (pages 61–64).

Read pages 6 and 7 of *World War I* to discover the causes of World War I. Complete "Causes of the Great War" (page 21).

Refer to the "Map of a Divided Europe" (page 20). Locate each of the countries. Ask students how they think the Central Powers got their name. Color code each country to signify which countries were part of the Central Powers, which were the Allies, and which countries remained neutral.

Watch the video "Secrets of the Unknown: The *Lusitania*." Discuss with students their opinions of the events that occurred when the *Lusitania* was hit.

Complete "The Sinking of the *Lusitania*" (page 22).

Journal Entry

The United States opted to stay neutral at the beginning of World War I, but Americans profited from the war by selling goods to European countries. What is your opinion on this? Was the United States truly neutral?

The United States was called *isolationist* because it did not want to get involved in international affairs. What are the pros and cons of being concerned only with your country? What role does the United States play today in the affairs of the world?

Chapters 5–8

Activities

What was the Sussex pledge? (*It was the promise Germany made to U.S. stating that it would abide by international law and not sink merchant or passenger ships without warning them. See page 33 in World War I.*) Have students describe it in their own words.

Using masking tape, tape down a square on the floor of your classroom that is just the size to fit each of your students in a sitting down position. Do not allow much room for movement. At the beginning of the lesson, ask all students to get within the square boundary you have made. Leave them in that position for at least five minutes. In time, ask students how they are feeling about their cramped conditions. Ask them to imagine that this area is also muddy, damp, and cold, and there are shots being fired at them. Then ask students to compare this activity to how the soldiers might have felt fighting in the trenches.

Look up the word "trench" in the dictionary. Ask students if they see any trenches being dug today. What are they used for?

Chapters 5–8 *(cont.)*

Have students draw an imaginary trench. How would they set up their trench? *(Answers will vary.)* What strategies might they use to protect themselves from the enemy? *(Answers will vary.)* How could they protect themselves from the weather and the elements? *(Answers will vary.)*

What does the word "attrition" mean? *(The act of weakening or exhausting by constant harassment or abuse.)*

Journal Entry

Do you think the United States should have joined World War I? Should it have waited so long after the *Lusitania* was sunk?

Was the threat of Mexico entering WWI a valid reason to become more involved in the events occurring in Europe?

Chapters 9–12

Activities

As a class, list the ways that the United States government enlisted the help, support, and confidence of the American people as they entered WWI. What strategies are still used today in political campaigns to convince people?

Have students design their own war bond posters *(see page 49 in World War I for more information, and see page 65 of this unit for war bond poster ideas.)*

The Selective Service Act was passed on May 18, 1917, to recruit an American armed force. What is the current feeling about the draft? *(Answers will vary.)* What was the feeling during other wars, such as the Vietnam War? *(There were strong anti-draft movements.)* Have students research events and issues related to the draft in America's recent history. Have students research the requirements of the Selective Service Act today.

How did the American soldiers receive the nickname "doughboy"?

America is a unique country in the sense that we are made up of citizens coming from other countries. What mistakes were made during this time with some of the German U.S. citizens? *(See page 50 in World War I.)* How can one determine loyalty?

Most of the popular songs written during this time period were written about the efforts and events of World War I. Complete the "Songs of World War I" music activity (page 23).

Journal Entry

If you were old enough to join the armed service in 1917, would you have volunteered to go to Europe to fight in World War I? What is your opinion of the Selective Service Act?

Why is it critical to have public support when fighting in a war? Can you think of examples when the government did not have public support for a war?

How do you feel about women fighting in the military?

World War I: Chapter Activities *(cont.)*

Chapters 13–16

Activities

What was the "American Expeditionary Force?"

Many new war weapons were used during World War I. Tanks, airplanes, U-boats, and machine guns all saw their place in World War I. How do inventions change our lives? Complete the "Mention My Invention" activity (page 24).

After an Allied victory due to the efforts of the American soldiers, Marine enlistments rose to 100% in two days. Why would victory prompt soldiers to join up?

As a class, discuss the conditions of the situation at Belleau Wood. Why was this battle so critical, especially since it did not allow its victor any needed ground?

What are mental battles? How do they affect attitude and confidence?

Second Lieutenant Frank "Balloon Buster" Luke became one of America's greatest aces during WWI. He was considered a hero. On pages 87–88 of *World War I*, read about the problems he had as well as his triumphs. Order in a large "hero" sandwich and spend lunch time together as a class discussing the characteristics of a good hero. Who are some heroes that students and teachers look up to today?

In these chapters, students begin to read accounts of soldiers seeing the value of human life degraded. This would be a good time to invite guest speakers to come in and talk with the class about the realities of war. Discuss how certain experiences that a person may have during war are with them for a lifetime.

Journal Entry

How did the United States make a difference in the events of World War I?

What do you think would have been the effect on America or the world today if the Allies had not won the war? How would the world be different if the Central Powers had gained control?

Think of a time in your life when you needed the help of someone else to accomplish something. Describe that experience in your journal and share it with a classmate.

Chapters 17–19

Activities

On page 90 of *World War I*, students read, "Each doughboy carried 200 rounds of ammunition, two cans of corned beef, six boxes of hardtack (Army biscuits) and one-quart canteen." These supplies hardly seemed enough to keep a soldier fighting strong. Experiment with this food by completing the "Cooking on the Western Front" activity (page 67). Also discuss with students the dire conditions mentioned on page 93 of *World War I*.

World War I: Chapter Activities *(cont.)*

Chapters 17–19 *(cont.)*

During the terrible battle of the Argonne, U.S. Major Charles Wittlesey used homing pigeons to signal to the American fighting lines that they were in need of help. Cher Ami was the most famous of these pigeons. Research homing pigeons and how they are trained. What are some other examples and stories of their efforts?

Chapter 18 relays the relief, joy, and satisfaction as the war ended in the 11th hour. The Yanks and the Germans met on middle ground and shared food and other items. Discuss as a class or in small groups how the feelings of war are hard to explain. Minutes before the cease fire, these soldiers would have immediately killed their "enemy"; minutes after, they communicated as acquaintances.

Journal Entry

How does war change things? Can things ever return to the way they were?

Have you experienced something in your life that you wish you could change back to the way it was? How does it make you feel? What are some of the ways that you deal with this feeling?

Chapters 20 and 21

Activities

The road home was a tough one for the soldiers stationed in Europe. While waiting to leave, many died of the influenza and other sicknesses. Complete "The Deadly Virus" activity (page 55) to learn more about contagious diseases.

To review the events and people of World War I, play the "World War I Quiz Game" as a class (pages 68 and 69).

Many lives were lost in World War I. Have students complete the "Graphing the Great War" activity on page 25 to demonstrate the number of lives that were lost.

What was the League of Nations? Research the League of Nations and the Fourteen Points offered by President Wilson. Is there anything like this in the world today?

Journal Entry

What are your thoughts and ideas about World War I now that you have studied it? World War I was called the "war to end all wars." Was it? Would it have been possible to prevent World War I? How did the results of World War I lead to World War II?

Important Dates of World War I

1914

June 28	The heir to the throne, Archduke Ferdinand Francis, was assassinated.
July 28	Austria-Hungary declared war on Serbia.
Aug. 1	Germany declared war on Russia.
Aug. 3	Germany declared war on France. Belgium was invaded by Germany. Great Britain declared war on Germany.
Sept. 1—Oct. 3	Austrians lost in the battle of Lemburg.
Oct. 30	Turkey joined the Central Powers.

1915

Feb. 18	Germany attempted a blockade of Great Britain.
April 22	Germans first used chloride poisonous gas.
May 7	A German submarine sank the British ship *Lusitania*.
May 23	Italy declared war on Austria-Hungary.

1916

Jan. 9	British troops withdrew from Gallipoli.
Feb. 21—Dec. 15	The Allies stopped the Germans in the Battle of Verdun.
April 29	Ten thousand British troops surrendered to the Turks.
June 4	Russia began an offensive in eastern Galicia.
July 1—Nov. 18	The Allies progressed in the Battles of the Somme.
Sept. 15	The British army first used tanks.

1917

Feb. 1	Germany first used submarine warfare.
April 6	The United States declared war on Germany.
June 26	The first American troops landed in France.
July 31—Aug. 9	The Germans broke up Russia's last offensive.
July 31—Nov. 10	The Germans stopped the Allies in the Third Battle of Ypres.
Nov. 7	The Bolsheviks took over Russia.
Nov. 20—Dec. 3	The Allies made the first tank attack in the Battle of Cambrai.
Dec. 9	Jerusalem fell to the Allies.
Dec. 15	Russia signed an armistice with Germany.

1918

Jan. 8	President Wilson revealed his "Fourteen Points" for peace.
March 3	Russia signed the Treaty of Brest-Litovsk. Allied forces were reduced.
March 21—June 15	Germany and Austria-Hungary fought the last great offensive.
Sept. 26	The Allies began their last attack on the western front.
Sept. 29	Bulgaria signed an armistice.
Oct. 30	The Ottoman Empire signed an armistice.
Nov. 3	Austria-Hungary signed an armistice.
Nov. 11	Germany signed the armistice. Fighting finally ended.

World War I Vocabulary

People

- Baker, Newton
- Bischoff, Major Hans Otto
- Bryan, William Jennings
- Catlin, Colonel Albertus
- Clemenceau, Georges
- Cohan, George M.
- Ferdinand, Archduke Franz
- Foch, General Ferdinand
- Gibson, Hugh
- Harbord, Brig. General James
- Kaiser, Wilhelm
- Lufberry, Raoul
- Luke, Frank
- Nicholas II, Czar of Russia
- Pershing, General John
- Petain, General Henri
- Rickenbacker, Eddie
- Sibley, Major Burton
- Turner, Captain William
- Wilson, Woodrow
- Wise, Colonel Frederick
- York, Sergeant Alvin

Places

- Argonne Forest
- Belleau Wood
- Caporetto
- Chateau-Thierry
- Gallipoli
- Louvain, Belgium
- Isonzo
- Jutland
- Paris, France
- Somme River
- St. Mihiel, France
- Verdun, France
- Versaille, France
- Ypres, France

Things

- Armistice
- Allies
- Communisim
- Central powers
- Tanks
- Machine gun
- Troops
- League of Nations
- Fourteen Points
- Storm Troopers
- Submarine/U-Boat
- Rations
- Trenches
- Chemical warfare
- War bonds
- Mess tent
- Ace pilots

Map of a Divided Europe

Locate each of the countries below on the map. Color the allied countries red, the central powers blue, and the neutral countries green.

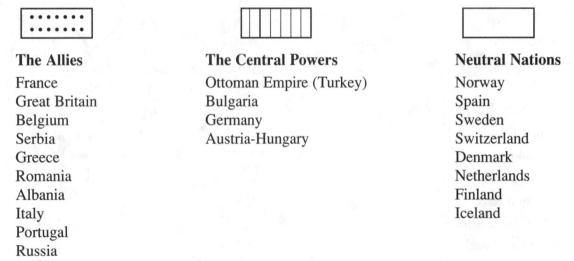

The Allies	**The Central Powers**	**Neutral Nations**
France	Ottoman Empire (Turkey)	Norway
Great Britain	Bulgaria	Spain
Belgium	Germany	Sweden
Serbia	Austria-Hungary	Switzerland
Greece		Denmark
Romania		Netherlands
Albania		Finland
Italy		Iceland
Portugal		
Russia		

Quick Question! Looking at your map, how do you think the Central Powers got that name?

Causes of the Great War

The causes of World War I have been noted as *nationalism*, *imperialism*, *militarism*, and the *system of alliances*. A brief definition of these causes is described below. After reading the definition, look on pages 5–7 of *World War I* and list examples of these causes.

Nationalism—when the citizens of a country exhibit strong loyalty and devotion to their nation

_____

_____

_____

_____

_____

_____

_____

Imperialism—the practice of extending the power and dominion of a country by acquiring territories and areas

_____

_____

_____

_____

_____

_____

_____

Militarism—when countries adopt a policy of aggressive military buildup to keep up with the militaries of neighboring countries

_____

_____

_____

_____

_____

System of Alliances—the repeated agreements that one country holds with another country. The interests of one country may align with another country in opposition to the interests of a third country.

_____

_____

_____

_____

_____

The Sinking of the *Lusitania*

The sinking of the *Lusitania*, a British passenger ship, was a pivotal event in World War I and led the United States to make some difficult decisions. Use resource books, encyclopedias, videos, and, if possible, people who lived during this time to piece the events together. Fill in the blanks of the news story below by using the words from the word bank.

Lusitania Sunk by German Submarine!

World War I began in _____ in the year _____ . During this

time, a passenger ship from _____ sailed out of a New York port to

_____ . Germany took out an advertisement in the _____ . It

said that all ships sailing under the British flag were subject to attack. Up until this time, passenger

ships had not been involved in the war. The *Lusitania* left on _____ and was

_____ hours late. The Captain of the *Lusitania* was _____ .

Lusitania was hit by a torpedo off the coast of _____ . The ship took

_____ minutes to sink. There was a second explosion on the *Lusitania*. Some say

that it was _____ being stored below deck, while others say that it was just the

_____ . Approximately _____ people lost their lives,

_____ were Americans. Many Americans were outraged and demanded that the

United States attack Germany. President Wilson responded by demanding that Germany stop attacking

passenger and merchant ships.

Word Bank

- Liverpool, England
- May 7, 1915
- 18
- 1914
- Ireland

- Europe
- 2
- Great Britain
- ammunition
- 124

- water heater
- 1200
- New York Times
- Captain Turner

Songs of World War I

The American soldiers came to Europe with enthusiasm and vigor.   The songs of this time period reflect feelings about sending American troops to foreign soil during turbulent times. Songs written about World War I were popular because they encouraged husbands, sons, and fathers that had left home to fight the war. Read the words of the famous song "Over There," written by George M. Cohen. This song was heard throughout the homes of America and on the battlefields of the Western front.

Over There
Over there, over there,
Spread the word, send the word, over there,
That the Yanks are coming, the Yanks are coming,
The drums, drum-drumming everywhere.
So prepare, say a prayer.
Send the word, spread the word to beware,
We'll be over, we're coming over,
And we won't come back till it's over, over there.

"You're in the Army Now!"   "I Didn't Raise My Boy to Be a Soldier"
"A Long Way to Tipperary"   "Roses of Picardy"
"Oh, How I Hate to Get Up in the Morning!"   "My Buddy"

Now write your own song to encourage the doughboys. What things can be put to song to bring cheer and comfort at such a fearful time?

_____
(Title)

_____

_____

_____

_____

_____

_____

_____

Mention My Invention

World War I Inventions

Inventions and improved inventions changed the story of World War I. Some of the inventions that played a role in the war included the submarine, the machine gun, the tank, and the airplane.

The submarine was given the name U-boat (from the German word for submarine, "unterseeboot"). Though the submarines were small and frail, a U-boat could fire from a small cannon and sink large passenger and supply ships. This halted the success of some countries in the war and determined the involvement of other countries in this war.

The idea of using airplanes in combat was at first unbelievable, but by the end of the war, combat planes earned their place in battle. At first, these planes were used for studying enemy plans and strategies. With improvement, these flying machines were used to shoot at the enemy from the air.

Each of these inventions played a critical role in the outcome of World War I, designed as the need arose.

You, too, can be an inventor! Look at your surroundings and discover ways to make things better, easier, or more efficient.

Invention Tips

To be a good inventor, use the following tips as guidelines:

- Take things apart to learn how they work.

- Be a researcher; learn about the origin and the history behind inventions.

- Watch people and animals at work. How do they do things?

- Learn from your mistakes.

- Think critically; learn to ask yourself questions and question the ideas of others.

- Keep trying! Your invention may not make sense today, but it might tomorrow.

Invention Evaluation

On a separate piece of paper, complete the questions below. Turn in your answers to your teacher for approval to go ahead and make your invention.

- Name of the invention

- Problem the invention solves

- Potential problems that might be caused by this invention

- The materials needed to make the invention

- What the invention looks like

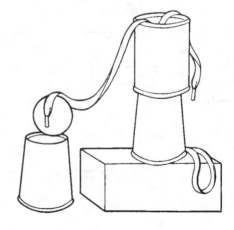

Graphing the Great War

By the end of the war, most families in France, Germany, and Great Britain had experienced the loss of a relative. In all, over 60 million men served in the militaries of World War I. No one will ever know the exact number of people who died as a result of the war, but here are the estimated numbers from the different countries:

Country	Estimated Deaths
Italy	0.5 million
Great Britain	1 million
France	1.4 million
Russia	1.7 million
Turkey	0.7 million
Austria	1.2 million
Germany	1.8 million

Using this data, create a bar graph in the space below. Be sure to give a title to your graph, and to label the horizontal and the vertical axes.

On a separate piece of paper, use the following information to create a line graph of the U-boat sinkings. Once you have finished, create five questions that can be answered by using your graph.

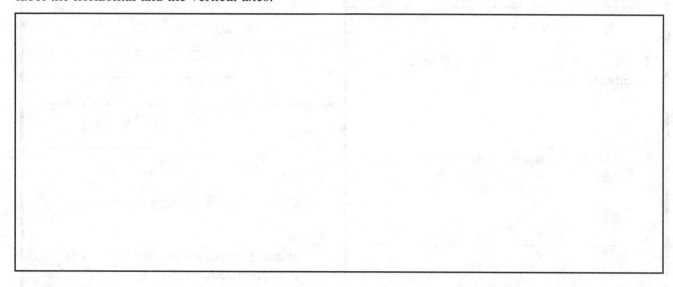

U-Boat Sinkings (in tons)

Year	Tons
1914	310,000
1915	1,301,000
1916	2,322,000
1917	6,270,000
1918	2,659,000

Causes and Effects of World War I

What were the causes and effects of World War I? Look at each statement below and fill in either the cause or effect that is missing. The first one has been done for you.

Causes	Effects
1. World War I caused countries to gain and lose power.	New European countries were created.
2. The United States wanted to defend democracy.	_____ _____ _____
3. _____ _____ _____	The League of Nations was formed.
4. The *Lusitania* was sunk by a German submarine.	_____ _____ _____
5. Archduke Ferdinand Francis was shot and killed.	_____ _____ _____
6. _____ _____ _____	Women supported the war by working in jobs previously held by men.
7. Germans used deadly gases for the first time in war.	_____ _____ _____
8. Many countries were committed to each other through their system of alliance.	_____ _____ _____

Fact or Opinion?

Directions: The statements below are facts and opinions. Please label each statement as fact (F) or opinion (O). Be prepared to defend your choice in class.

1. _____ The United States entered the war in 1917.

2. _____ Germany was about to win the war just as the United States became involved.

3. _____ Archduke Ferdinand Francis was shot and killed.

4. _____ Machine guns and other new weapons were introduced during World War I.

5. _____ Americans thought that fighting in World War I would defend democracy.

6. _____ Women helped the United States win the war.

7. _____ Before the United States got into the war, its government didn't care what happened in Europe.

8. _____ Nationalism was one of the causes of World War I.

9. _____ World War I enabled the United States to become a world power.

10. _____ The Selective Service Act became law on May 18, 1917.

11. _____ Because of strong anti-German feelings, German-Americans tried to prove their loyalty by purchasing war bonds and changing the name "sauerkraut" to "liberty cabbage."

12. _____ Before World War I, America's army numbered fewer than 200,000 men and was ranked only 17th in the world.

After the Dancing Days

by Margaret I. Rostkowski

Summary

This is the story of a young girl, Annie, and her family, who struggle with the tragedies of World War I. After Annie loses her favorite uncle, Paul, during fighting in World War I, she questions facts about her uncle's death, sending her on a search for the truth. As a result, Annie leaves the protective cloak of childhood and sees the realities of the adult world. Along the way, she befriends a veteran who was disfigured from the mustard gas used during the World War I. Her first reaction to the veteran was fear, but with time, friendship blossoms between them. In the end, Annie learns the true meaning of friendship and comes to understand the struggles many war veterans face as they return to the country which they defended.

Each of the lessons suggested below may take from one to several days to complete.

Sample Plan

Lesson 1

- ❏ Introduce *After the Dancing Days* with "Setting the Stage" (page 29).
- ❏ Assemble literature logs and set up discussion groups (page 33).
- ❏ Assign reading pages for each day and have students sign the "Student Agreement Form" (page 35).
- ❏ Complete the following:
  "Charting the Feelings Graph" (page 44)
  Read Chapters 1–5 of *After the Dancing Days*.
  Begin "Daily Literature Log" assignments (pages 36–38).

Lesson 2

- ❏ Read Chapters 6–10 in *After the Dancing Days*
- ❏ Continue "Daily Literature Log" assignments (pages 36–38).
- ❏ Complete "Wearing a Scar" (page 40).

Lesson 3

- ❏ Read Chapters 11–15 in *After the Dancing Days*.
- ❏ Continue "Daily Literature Log" assignments (pages 36–38).
- ❏ Complete "Vocabulary Ventures" (page 39).

Lesson 4

- ❏ Read Chapters 16–20 in *After the Dancing Days*.

- ❏ Continue "Daily Literature Log" assignments (pages 36–38).
- ❏ Complete the following:
  "Say Something!" (page 41)
  "Piecing It Together!" (page 42)
  "World War I Math Problems" (page 54)

Lesson 5

- ❏ Read Chapters 21–25 in *After the Dancing Days*.
- ❏ Continue "Daily Literature Log" assignments (pages 36–38).
- ❏ Complete the following:
  "Tour de France" (page 43)
  "Deadly Gases (page 56)
  "Events of the Great War" (page 58)
  "Dilemma—A Time for Making Decisions" (page 66)

Lesson 6

- ❏ Read Chapters 26–30 in *After the Dancing Days*.
- ❏ Continue "Daily Literature Log" assignments (pages 36–38).
- ❏ Complete the following:
  "Story Map" (page 45)
  "Coordinating the Points" (page 52)
  "Solve the Puzzle" (page 46)
  "Critical Thinking" (pages 47 and 48)
  "Author for a Day" (see Extending the Book, page 31)
  "In the Spotlight"
  (see Extending the Book, page 32).

Overview of Activities

Setting the Stage

1. Assemble the "World War I: The War to End All Wars" bulletin board using the historical fiction stories written by the students (page 73).

2. Put together "Literature Logs" and discuss each section with the students (pages 36–38).

3. Read the "Student Agreement Form" (page 35) and have students sign the form.

4. Read the picture book *Casey Over There* by Rabin Staton and Greg Shed (Harcourt Brace, 1997). Discuss as a class the emotions caused when a family member leaves to fight. Ask class members if they know anyone close to them that has fought in a war. What types of feelings did they experience? Explain to the students that this book takes place after the ending of World War I.

5. Discuss with the students the meaning of the title *After the Dancing Days*. What is a dance? What types of emotions are associated with dancing? What might be meant by "after the dancing days" in relation to World War I? Tell the students that this is a story about a young girl who struggles with losing an uncle during the war while anxiously awaiting her father's return from the battlefield and who meanwhile meets a disfigured veteran. The story is about the days after the end of World War I and how these characters worked to put their lives back together.

Enjoying the Book

1. Assign pages to be read each day as suggested on the "Student Agreement Form" (page 35).

2. After completing the daily reading assignment, students can complete the discussion questions, and journal questions in their literature logs. Students need to be prepared with all materials and assignments for the daily discussion groups.

3. Begin "Charting the Feelings" (page 44), an activity that will be added to as the students read the book. Allow time for students to add to their chart during the daily discussion group.

4. Complete "Wearing a Scar" (page 40). Discuss with students the meaning of the word "hero." Are war veterans considered heroes? Are they treated as heroes? Even those who may have been injured and lead very difficult lives after the war? Why do people love the fanfare, the parades, and the excitement of winning a war, but fear the realities, or scars, of war? This activity gives students the opportunity to explore the feelings associated with living with and associating with those who have permanent visible scars or injuries.

5. "Vocabulary Ventures" (page 39) expands the vocabulary of the students and increases their dictionary skills. As an extension, have students write a story using at least five of these vocabulary words, or play the vocabulary game where all vocabulary words are written on a sticky note, and then placed on the back of each student in the classroom. Students then have to ask "yes" or "no" questions and may not use any of the vocabulary words to figure out which words are stuck to their backs.

Overview of Activities (cont.)

Enjoying the Book (cont.)

6. All students have had disagreements with their parents before. Now take a closer look at the disagreement the character Annie had with her mother. Should Annie be allowed to visit Andrew or not? Put 15 red blocks and 15 blue blocks (or similar item found in your classroom) in a bowl. Designate one color to be the side of the parents and the other color be the side of the children. Have students draw to find out which side they belong to. Explain how to have an objective point of view, even though they may not agree with the side they have been assigned. Discuss with your class how they can discuss the issue. Establish rules for debate such as the following:

   • Flip a coin to see which side begins.

   • Give each side two minutes to make a statement and two minutes to respond.

   • Require that only designated members of the group may speak during the discussion/response time.

   • Select a student to be the moderator/time keeper.

7. "Say Something!" is a strategy to discuss and review what was read in a story (page 41). In small discussion groups, take turns reading each section and pausing at each spot that is designated with an asterisk (*). Students may then spontaneously respond to the sentences just read.

8. Just like a puzzle, we read stories and pieces from books that reflect events from our lives. Copy "Piecing It Together" (page 42) for students to complete. This page may be done in class or as a homework assignment.

9. Sharpen your students' research skills with the activity "Tour de France" (page 43). Students may work with a partner or individually. Allow plenty of time in your classroom to complete and present projects.

10. While students are reading, or after the book has been read, recall story events with the class by completing the Story Map on page 45. Just as you use a map to travel to a chosen destination, a story map is a useful technique that helps students "walk through" a story they have read. It helps cement comprehension and allows the teacher a chance to teach story elements such as characters, setting, and plot. This activity may be done individually, in small groups, or together as a class.

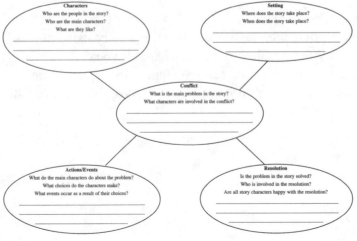

Overview of Activities *(cont.)*

Enjoying the Book *(cont.)*

11. Review events of World War I with "World War I Math Problems" (page 54) that students can solve in pairs or individually. The page contains geometry problems using formulas to find perimeter, area, and volume. After students have finished the problems, assign each problem to a different student or pair of students to teach to the class. They should work through each problem step-by-step and should answer any questions that other students might have.

12. Research the toxic gases used in World War I and their effects on the human body (page 56). Provide students with access to science books, encyclopedias, library books, videos, guest speakers, or other resources to gather this information.

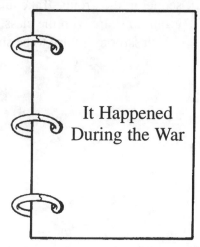

Extending the Book

1. Invite individuals to come to talk to your class about World War I. There are many families that had relatives involved that could come and share their ancestors' experiences, newspaper clippings, maps, medals, journals, etc. These are the best ways to teach students the reality about the war. Allow students to ask questions and to learn more about how things were. A good source of information might also be somebody who works with veterans' organizations or support groups.

2. Solve the puzzle on page 46 with World War I terms and *After the Dancing Days* vocabulary words. Have an answer page completed and on hand for students to check their own work when they are finished.

3. Distribute "Coordinating the Points" (page 52) to your students. Review coordinate points before beginning this activity.

4. Encourage your students to read as many books written about World War I as possible to broaden their understanding of this time period in world history. Lead them to discover that each character experiences the war differently. Once students have completed several books, create a "Mural of Memories" about them. Begin the mural by taping a large sheet of butcher paper to a door or bulletin board. Make colored paper available to the students for printing the title, the author, and a description and/or illustration of the book they read.

5. Allow students to act as an author for a day! Give students the opportunity to write a historical fiction story set in World War I. Pair students up to edit each other's work. Publish the stories in a book using tagboard, construction paper, or thick paper for a cover and yarn, staple, or rings as a binding. Hold a class contest to vote on their favorite story. Share the stories with other classes or students.

It Happened During the War

Overview of Activities *(cont.)*

Extending the Book *(cont.)*

6. "In the Spotlight!" is an interactive experience that allows students to show the knowledge that they have learned about the book *After the Dancing Days*. Divide your class into groups. Each group is responsible for becoming an "expert" on *After the Dancing Days* by reviewing and studying the book. The group that is "in the spotlight" should arrange their chairs in a semi-circle at the front of the room. Audience members then take turns asking questions of the group. As each question is asked, group members have one minute to put their heads together and answer the question. The student who asked the question then selects a member of the group to answer the question, so that each group member must be prepared. After the group answers five questions, a new group becomes "spotlighted." The game continues until each group has had a turn.

7. Meet one last time in discussion groups. Discuss the students' feelings about the book. Were their predictions about the book correct? Were there any surprises in the book? What was their favorite part? Would the students wish to change anything?

8. Allow students to choose at least one activity to complete from each category in the "Critical Thinking" (pages 47 and 48). This will allow the student to clarify their understanding of the story. Using Bloom's taxonomy allows the teacher to evaluate the understanding and comprehension of the students at different levels. Copy pages 47–48 back to back and distribute to students. Some of these activities can be done with a small group, with a partner, and individually. Be sure each student reports to you on the finished product.

9. Review events of World War I and their place in history. As a homework assignment, send students home with "Events of the Great War" (page 58). As they come in the next day, have the answers posted on the door or chalkboard.

10. Every day, we must make decisions. Each wartime leader involved in WWI made decisions that led to the events and outcomes of WWI. As a class, discuss problem-solving strategies. Use "Dilemma—A Time for Making Decisions" (page 66) for some suggestions.

11. In discussion groups, have each student begin writing the sequel to *After the Dancing Days*. After students have written at least two paragraphs, have each one pass his or her paper to the student sitting to the right. Students read the new page in front of them and add to this sequel. Continue rotating in the same order until each student has had an opportunity to add to each sequel in the group. Take turns sharing the sequels. Vote on the favorite from the discussion group to share with the class. Bind all of the sequels in a notebook or binder and store them in the classroom library to be shared by all the students.

32

Literature Log and Discussion Group Guide

Literature Log

A literature log is a place where students document their learning as they read a literature book. It keeps all of the students' assignments and journal entries in one place. It allows the student and teacher to look back at the progress the student has made from the beginning to the end of the literature book.

To make a literature log, each student needs a notebook that is divided into at least two sections. Have students label one section "Discussion Group" and one section "Journal." This is called a literature log.

Student Agreement Form

Review the "Student Agreement Form" (page 35), making certain that each student understands his or her responsibilities for reading the assignments, answering discussion questions, completing activities, and answering journal questions.

Discussion Group

Divide your class into small groups. After each reading assignment is completed, these groups will meet together to discuss the reading and the discussion questions assigned. Select a student to assume the role of monitor. The monitor may be a different student each day or you may select a student to always be the monitor. The monitor is to ensure that each member of the group has the opportunity to contribute and participate each day.

During the first discussion group, show the students the book *After the Dancing Days*. Find out information about the author and see if she has written any other books. Discuss with students what they think the story might be about. Spend time as a group discussing the role of the monitor and all of the students' responsibilities to the discussion group. (See "Rules of the Discussion Group," below.) Then spend time setting up the literature logs, explaining to the students that at the end of the book, this log will be turned in for review and grading.

Rules of the Discussion Group

Write these on a large piece of paper and post them near the discussion group table.

1. All members of the group must be on task and participating.

2. Each person must complete the reading assignment.

3. Each person must come prepared with his or her literature log, a copy of *After the Dancing Days*, a pencil, and any other requested items.

4. No "put downs" or negative comments are allowed.

5. Each person must listen to the other members of his or her group.

Literature Log and Discussion Group Guide *(cont.)*

Questions to ask yourself:

- Do I listen to other members of the group?
- Do I show my attention by looking at the teacher and responding?
- Do I ask for clarification when I don't understand?
- Do I contribute to the discussion? too much? too little?
- Do I speak to all members of the group, not just the monitor or the teacher?
- Do I speak clearly and loudly enough for all to hear?
- Do I encourage others to speak?

Discussion Group Activities

Under the reading assignment for each day (pages 36–38), there are activities listed. These activities may be done individually or as a discussion group. A teacher may also assign the following activities to be done in the discussion group.

Begin the first discussion group explaining the "Charting the Feelings" activity (page 44). This should take place during each subsequent discussion group. These can be kept in a folder near the table where the discussion group meets.

Have students make predictions for the next reading assignment.

Choose a scene from the book to illustrate and see if other discussion members can name the scene.

Assign each group member a character from the group and have them role play scenes from the book. These can be presented to other discussion groups.

Give each member an index card in which to write down an event from the story. Then, place all the index cards in a pile and have group members sequence them in order.

Ask each student to prepare questions from the assigned reading to test the knowledge of the other members of the group.

Have students trace their hands on a piece of paper. Then have them select characters from the book. On each finger of the hand, students can write different traits about each character. These hands could be placed around the room or on a bulletin board entitled "Give Them a Hand!"

Place all the names of the main characters in a hat and have each student in the discussion group draw a name. Stage a mock interview and have students respond to questions as their characters would.

Journal Questions

In the second section of their notebooks, students can write their journal entries. After each reading assignment and discussion questions (pages 36–38), there are journal questions for the students' responses. Students must answer in complete sentences. Journal answers or responses may also be shared in the discussion group if time allows. Journal questions might be good homework assignments to complete after the reading and discussion questions are answered in class.

Student Agreement Form

I,_____, agree to read *After the Dancing Days*, written by Margaret I. Rostkowski. This book has a total of 217 pages. Each day I need to answer discussion questions, do activities, and answer journal questions. I will use the following chart to help me keep track of assignments assigned by my teacher:

Day	Reading Assignment	Discussion Questions	Activities	Journal Questions
Day One	Chapters 1–5			
Day Two	Chapters 6–10			
Day Three	Chapters 11–15			
Day Four	Chapters 16–20			
Day Five	Chapters 21–25			
Day Six	Chapters 26–30			

Literature Log Assignments

Chapters 1–5

Discussion

What things have changed since Annie's father left two years ago? *(Annie's routines have changed, Annie has gotten closer to her mother.)* Why does Annie feel left out at her father's homecoming? *(Her father is getting accustomed to being home and seeing everyone so that Annie feels ignored.)* Why do family members seem to have forgotten about Annie's Uncle Paul? *(Annie's family is trying to forget the pain they feel about his death so do not bring up the subject.)*

Journal Entry

In Chapter Four, Annie remembers a special night she shared with Uncle Paul before he left for war. Have you ever shared a moment like this with someone special? What did you do? Why was it so important? Do you still have a relationship with this person?

Extension

Research the types of organizations or services that are available for returning veterans, for example, the Disabled American Veterans *(DAV)*. What types of support services are offered?

Chapters 6–10

Discussion

Annie's mother struggles with the subject of injured soldiers. Why do you think it is hard for her to deal with it? *(Some people have a harder time dealing with serious accidents, illness, and death. Annie's mother might also feel upset when she thinks that this might have occrred to her brother.)* What is Annie's reaction to meeting Andrew for the first time? *(She is scared, stunned, and speechless.)* Andrew reacts angrily. Why? *(Andrew is angry about the things that have happened to his life. He might also be afraid of being rejected and puts up a defensive wall to avoid feeling hurt by others.)*

Journal Entry

How do you feel about being around somebody who has been badly injured? What do you do when you see someone in a wheelchair, someone who is blind, etc.?

Extension

Research the League of Nations. What was this group and what were its goals?

Research statues in memory of soldiers who have fought and died for our country, e.g., "The Unknown Soldier" or "The Wall." Read *The Wall*, written by Eve Bunting and illustrated by Ronald Himler, as a class or in discussion groups. Discuss the feelings associated with such memorials.

Literature Log Assignments *(cont.)*

Chapters 11–15

Discussion

This story is written from Annie's point of view. How might the story be different if it was written from Annie's mother's point of view? Her father's? Andrew's? *(Answers will vary.)* Annie has chosen to lie to her parents. Is she doing the right thing? Why? *(Answers will vary.)*

Journal Entry

Assume the character of Annie and write a letter in your journal as though you were she. What might feelings might you express? How have things changed in your life? What are you thinking about your mother and the fight that you had? *(Answers will vary.)*

Chapters 16–20

Discussion

Why do you think there is no Purple Heart in Uncle Paul's collection of medals? *(Students need to make a prediction.)* Why did Annie's father lie to her about the returning soldiers? *(Her father was trying to protect Annie from the horrible results of war.)* What is the significance of Andrew talking about someone else's injuries instead of his own for a change? *(Once we begin to help others, we do not feel so sorry for ourselves and we feel better.)* What did Andrew and Annie find out about her Uncle Paul's death? *(They find out that he couldn't have died fighting in battle because of the conflict in the date listed in the telegram.)* Timothy goes to have his bandages taken off. What is the result? *(Timothy can see.)* Who arrives home? *(Annie's mother unexpectedly returns.)*

Journal Entry

Tell about a time you received an award, certificate, medal, or trophy. How did you feel about it when you got it? How do you feel about it today?

Extension

List all of the important characters in the book. Now state the following facts about them: name, age, personality traits, appearance, occupation, feelings about other characters. Support your conclusions with details of characterization from the book.

Research the Purple Heart award. Where did it originate? What are the qualifications to receive one? How is one presented with a Purple Heart?

Literature Log Assignments *(cont.)*

Chapters 21–25

Discussion:

What information did Lt. Owen provide? *(Lt. Owen told Annie's family that Annie's Uncle Paul died as a result of not having medication for the measles. He was left in a corner with a high fever while injured soldiers were brought in to be cared for.)* Why did Annie's mother change her mind about Annie going to the hospital? *(She talked it over with Annie's father and realized how important this was to him and to Annie. She is still not comfortable with it, but she realizes that she needs to let Annie do this.)* Why was it upsetting to find out how Uncle Paul died in World War I? *(They felt sad that Uncle Paul was left alone to die without anybody being able to help him.)* What are some of the changes in Andrew? *(He begins to help other patients in the hospital. He becomes thoughtful and more considerate of others.)* How does Annie feel about the changes? *(She is hurt because she sees Andrew's desire to help other people as a way of saying that he doesn't have time to spend with her.)* Why does Andrew's happiness make Annie feel sad? *(She feels she is losing a friend.)* Who comes to visit Annie? *(Mrs. Crayton, Andrew's mother.)* What are Andrew's latest plans? *(He will be taking a job at a hospital in Topeka.)* Why does Annie react the way she does? *(She is hurt by Andrew's decision to leave.)* How has Andrew and Annie's relationship changed? *(Answers will vary.)*

Journal Entry

Andrew tells Annie, "You're a good thing for me." Why? Who are some people in your life who have been good or bad influences? What is your influence on other people?

Chapters 26–30

Discussion

How old do you think Annie is? Why do you think so? Document your answer with excerpts from the text.

What did Annie give to Andrew? *(An atlas of the United States to help him find his way.)* What did Andrew give to Annie? *(His Purple Heart.)*

Journal Entry

What did you think of the book? Why? Write a letter to the author, Margaret Rostkowski, telling her your feelings.

Extension

Create a Venn diagram of Annie and Andrew's characters. In what ways are they alike? In what ways are they different?

Vocabulary Ventures

Directions: Read and complete each section below.

A.   Listed below are vocabulary words and the pages on which they can be found in *After the Dancing Days*. Look up the words in the novel and define them in your own words using the context clues. Then match the vocabulary word to its dictionary definition in Part B.

Vocabulary Words	**What I think they mean:**
loose shift (page 58)	1. _____
tufts (page 58)	2. _____
sullen (page 85)	3. _____
lulled (page 92)	4. _____
sultry (page 98)	5. _____
skittered (page 99)	6. _____
gallant (page 105)	7. _____
cicadas (page 85)	8. _____
platoon (page 144)	9. _____

10._____   brave, often self-sacrificing

11._____   hot and humid

12._____   soft, comfortable dress

13._____   caused to sleep or rest

14._____   moved quickly about

15._____   of a military unit

16._____   cluster

17._____   with stout bodies, wide blunt heads, and large transparent wings

18._____   resentfully quiet

B.   Read each sentence below from *After the Dancing Days* and then rewrite it, replacing the vocabulary word with another word (or words) that means the same thing.

I pulled up several *tufts* of browning grass._____

"I never did anything *gallant*," he said._____

She fanned herself, moving the *sultry* air around her face._____

Grandmother *skittered* about him, moving furniture that wasn't in the way, pulling at the shawl that hung around his neck, repeating his name over and over.

C.   On a separate sheet of paper, use each vocabulary word from Part A in your own sentence.

Wearing a Scar

Andrew was injured while fighting in World War I and returned home a wounded veteran with disfigured face and hands. His personality is different, too, as he seems angry with everyone. In the book, Annie adjusts to how Andrew looks, but it wasn't always that way.

In the book we read the following:

[I] dropped the book bag over the high back. Someone was already sitting there. He turned.

I felt as if I had been hit in the face. For a moment I couldn't breathe.

The only thing normal about him was his eyes, but even they were pulled out of shape. The rest of his face was red, as if it had been deeply sunburned, and all of his features were pulled downward, as if hot tears had run down and melted his face. His mouth had no lips. It looked as if someone had cut a slit where his mouth should be.

We stared at each other, I holding to the back of the bench, he half-turned away from me.

I wanted to turn and run away, not in space, but in time, to the moment before I had seen him. And then I did run . . . I stood, my hands clenched in front of my eyes, waiting for the image of that face to fade.

Now choose one of the following questions. Write a paragraph to answer it. Once finished, edit your paragraph to ensure correct spelling, punctuation, and capitalization.

- What types of things does a person who has been disfigured or badly injured need to have and do in order to work through the immense changes in his or her life?

- Why do those who are hurt often act angry and hostile to those who offer love and support?

- How does life change for the family members of those who were injured? In what ways do these family members need support and love?

_____

_____

_____

_____

_____

_____

_____

_____

_____

Say Something!

Say Something! is a strategy used to discuss and review what is read in a story. Below are excerpts taken from *After the Dancing Days*. Read aloud the following paragraphs as a class. Whenever there is an asterisk (*), students are allowed to say something that comes to mind as they are reading this section. More than one student may contribute to the discussion. After thoughts and ideas are shared, the reading is continued. Comments on the character and his/her actions, the setting, the plot, the author, World War I, etc., are all welcomed into the discussion.

Conversation #1

"Thank you, Annie. You're a wise young lady. I'm so glad you could join me this evening. For many reasons." And then he kissed my hand.

"I am too. Thank you." *

I thanked him again when he brought me to the door of our house, thanked him and told him I would never forget this evening.

. . . Mother was waiting for me in the living room. When I told her about the opera and was unable to explain how wonderful it all was, she said she knew.

"And how was Uncle Paul? Did he treat you right?"

"Oh yes. He acted like I was . . . like I was a lady." *

Mother tipped back her head and laughed. "How nice of him. Paul has his faults, but he is a gentleman. I tell you, Annie, there are advantages to having such young uncles. You'll appreciate it before you're much older." *

But Uncle Paul enlisted in the army before I got much older.

Conversation #2

Grandfather read on, finishing one chapter and starting another. I got tired of the hard bench and had to stretch out on the cool grass beside Andrew, plucking grass. At first I didn't notice Mother when she came and stood on the edge of our little circle. Grandfather saw her first. *

"Katherine! What a nice surprise! Come, pull up a bench." Mother looked at him, at me, at Timothy, and her lips tightened. Andrew stood up and she turned and looked at him. Her face grew pale. She swung back to me. "Annie, get your things now." *

I got to my feet. "Mother, I want you to meet ———"

"Now, Annie. I'll meet you at the car. Coming, Father?" *

Conversation #3

"Eric, how did my uncle die? Do you know?" *

He didn't move for a minute, and I moved my hand forward to touch his arm. Then he looked back at me. "I was with him. They let me stay with him, even though he didn't know me at the end. He was burning up, delirious . . ."*

"They said they couldn't do anything for him. Just then, the hospital began to get the wounded Marines from the front. So they put him in a corner. . . ." *

Eric moved his head back and forth on the pillow, "No, no, he wasn't wounded. He was sick. Measles." *

Piecing It Together

When we read, our minds bring the story to life. We visualize scenes and experiences that the characters are having. Often we can relate to the character and his or her experiences because we have experienced similar events.

Choose there experiences from this book and describe them on the chart below. Then, describe similar experiences you have had in your life and how it was similar to that of the character's experience. The first one has been done for you.

An interesting part in the book . . .

1. Annie's Uncle Paul takes her out for a special night at the opera. She is flattered that he wanted to take her, just a young girl. Annie is treated like a lady and feels as if she were in heaven.

2. _____
   _____
   _____
   _____

3. _____
   _____
   _____
   _____

4. _____
   _____
   _____
   _____

This reminds me of this time in my life . . .

When I was 12, I thought my big brother was so cool! He was five years older than I was, but one night he took me to the town football game and let me sit with him and all of his older friends. I felt really important.

_____
_____
_____
_____

_____
_____
_____
_____

_____
_____
_____
_____

Tour de France

Annie was fascinated with other countries and was interested in traveling across the world. In *After the Dancing Days* we read, "I began to dream of taking such trips after the first talk with Ruth, of drifting down the rivers I traced on the maps, of meeting veiled strangers in Kashmir or Samarkand, and they would never have seen someone like me and they would take me to the palace to meet the prince and . . .

After Uncle Paul left, I began to study the map of Europe more carefully. I found LeHavre where he would have landed, the Somme River near where he was based, Paris, and the Ile de France. And my dreams changed. Now I was there in France, a nurse helping the wounded, risking death to care for a soldier with dark eyes."

Take a book trip to France. Use encyclopedias, the computer, and collect books from the library and read about France. Here are some places in France to investigate:

- Paris
- Chateau-Thierry
- Verdun
- Rheims
- Loire River
- Ardennes Forest
- Lille
- Versailles
- Marne River
- Belleau Wood
- Seine River
- Versailles

Points to cover in my project on France:

- What do I want to teach others about France? (List all ideas.)
- How do I want to present this information? (List all the project ideas in which you are interested.)
- What is my plan? (List step-by-step the order in which you will complete your project.)
- What encyclopedias, books, videos, computer sources, and other information will I use?
- Have I included a bibliography of all the sources of information that I used?

Once you have gathered this material, choose two of the following:

_____ Write a children's book about France.

_____ Write a letter home telling about your journey to France.

_____ Decorate the flag of France and learn the meaning of its colors.

_____ Design and color a travel brochure of France.

_____ Write a reader's theater script to be presented in front of the class, telling about your trip to France.

_____ Compare and contrast France with United States. How is it different? How is it the same?

_____ Interview an imaginary or real person from France. What questions would you ask to help you learn about France?

_____ Create a game that teaches the players information about France.

Charting the Feelings

Chart Annie's feelings from the beginning of the book to the end. At the end of each chapter or group of chapters, write down an incident that takes place and chart how she is feeling about it on a scale of 1 to 10, (1 meaning not stressful and 10 meaning stressful) rate the events. Some of the issues include her father's return, the effects of World War I, meeting Andrew and the other soldiers, the loss of her uncle, the questions about her uncle's death, and her changing relationship with her mom. An example has been done for you.

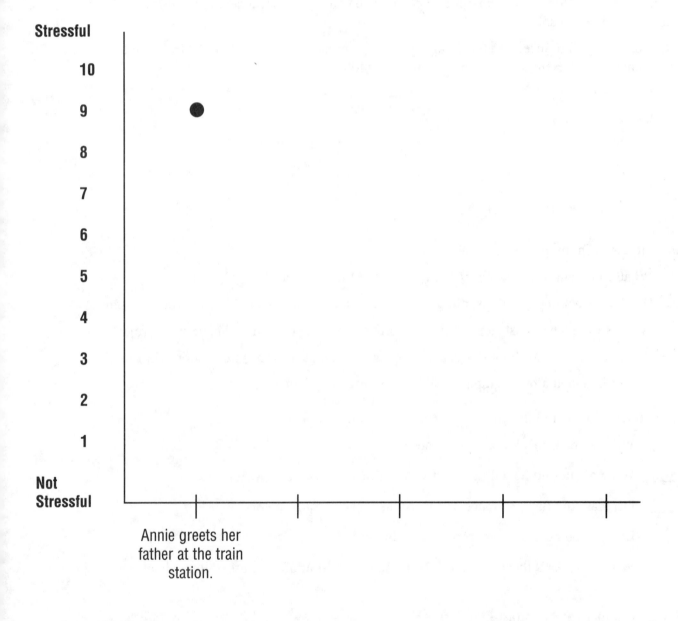

Stressful

10
9 ●
8
7
6
5
4
3
2
1

Not Stressful

Annie greets her father at the train station.

Think About It!

What are Annie's feelings? Look at the events that were rated high (stressful). Can you find a pattern, such as the same people being involved in events that are stressful?

Story Map

Map out the story of Annie and her experiences in *After the Dancing Days* on the form below.

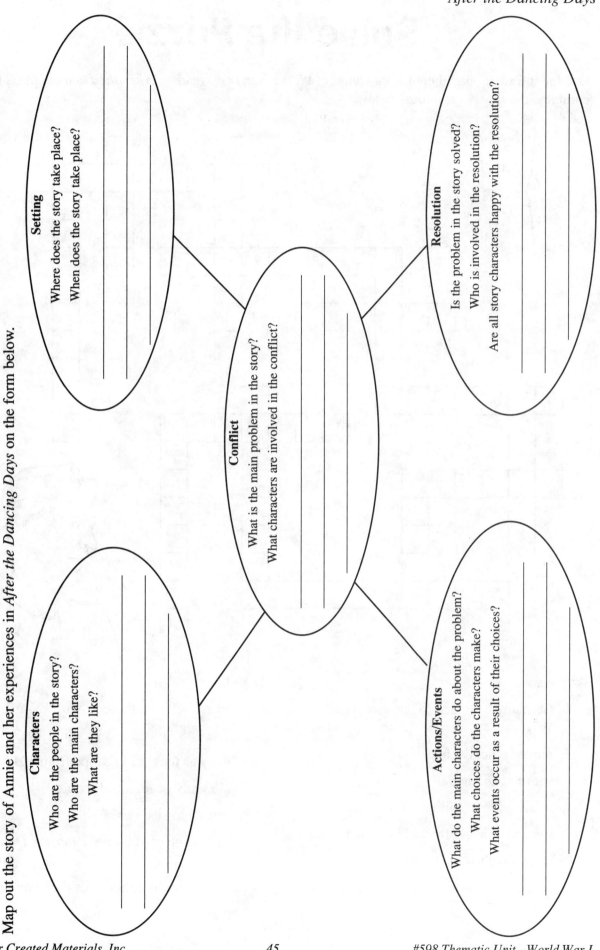

Setting

Where does the story take place?

When does the story take place?

Resolution

Is the problem in the story solved?

Who is involved in the resolution?

Are all story characters happy with the resolution?

Conflict

What is the main problem in the story?

What characters are involved in the conflict?

Characters

Who are the people in the story?

Who are the main characters?

What are they like?

Actions/Events

What do the main characters do about the problem?

What choices do the characters make?

What events occur as a result of their choices?

Solve the Puzzle

Use the information gathered from studying World War I and reading *After the Dancing Days* to complete the crossword puzzle below.

Across

4. Germany belonged to this group during WWI.
5. moved quickly about
6. very hot and humid
7. subdivision of military unit
12. spirited, brave, often self-sacrificing
10. insects with stout bodies
14. soft, comfortable dress

Down

1. Many suffered these in World War I.
2. The U.S. joined this group in 1917.
3. the war fought in Europe from 1914–1918
5. gloomily or resentfully quiet
8. caused to sleep or rest
9. first name of author of *After the Dancing Days*
11. brave people fighting for their country
13. clumps or clusters

46

Critical Thinking

Knowledge

1. Write down the names of each character and draw a picture of what they might look like.

2. Draw a picture of a scene from the story and write what happened on the back.

3. Create a word search or crossword puzzle using the characters from the story.

4. In a small group, have one student describe a character while other students guess who it is.

5. Write down five sentences about an event from the story on a piece of paper. Cut up the sentences and mix them up. Switch with a partner and put each other's sentences in the correct order.

   I will complete #_____.

Comprehension

1. Choose a partner. Each of you should draw five pictures of events from the story. Then use each other's scenes to describe what has happened in the story.

2. Recall the story in your own words. Record your version on a cassette tape and listen to your story.

3. Describe an event from the story and ask a partner to draw a picture of what happened next. Do the same with the event he or she chooses.

4. Create a time line of events from the story using brief information and a small illustration for each event.

5. Have a partner write down five key words from the story, then explain the meaning these words had in the story. Switch and have your partner explain your chosen key words. (A key word, for example, might be "mustard gas," which could be explained as having been used in the story to explain what happened to Andrew during WWI.)

   I will complete #_____.

Application

1. Choose one of the problems a character had in the story and write in your own words about a similar problem you have had. How did you and the character go about solving the problems?

2. Make puppets or dress up like the characters and act out a scene from the story.

3. Select a situation from the story and write down how the character could have done things differently.

4. Take one of the characters from this story and place him or her in a different story. How would this character have acted, spoken, and made decisions in the new story?

   I will do #_____.

Critical Thinking *(cont.)*

Analysis

1. From this historical fiction book, discuss and write down the events that are fiction and the parts that are nonfiction.

2. List all of the main characters and as many characteristics as you can think of for each character.

3. Select two characters from the story. Draw a Venn diagram and place the names of each character on either side. Compare and contrast the two characters.

4. Select one of the characters and write down his or her daily schedule. What would he or she do? What would he or she eat? Where would he or she go?

   I will do number # _____.

Synthesis

1. Select a different title for the book, one that would give a good idea of what the novel is about. Then create a new cover for the book.

2. Write a poem that one of the main characters would have written to express his/her ideas, thoughts, and opinions.

3. Design a poster to advertise the book. Be sure to include names of characters and information that would entice one to read the book. Use bright colors and bold letters.

4. Add a new character to the plot. How does this character change the story?

   I will do # _____.

Evaluation

1. Compare this story with another one you have read. Create a Venn diagram and compare and contrast the two stories. Select another book about World War I to use for this activity.

2. Select one of the characters that you would like to get to know better. Write him or her a letter inviting him or her to come to your class for a day. Explain to the character why you would be interested in their visit.

3. Form a small group and discuss the different characters in the book. How do you feel about each character? Did you agree with the actions that each character took? How do you think they should have done things differently?

4. Write a letter to Margaret Rostkowski, the author of *After the Dancing Days*, and tell her your thoughts and ideas about the story. Rate the story in comparison to other books you have read on the subject.

   I will do # _____.

World War I Poetry

Poetry is a form of written expression that can bring thoughts and feelings to life through unique language sounds and verbal images. Many people enjoy reading and listening to the rhythm of poetry and visualizing images that poetry creates. Different types of poems fit different types of occasions. A "word cinquain" allows descriptions and ideas to be written about in an organized fashion. Use the following guideline for a word cinquain:

Line 1:	Title	1 word
Line 2:	Description of title	2 words
Line 3:	Action about the title	3 words
Line 4:	Feeling about the title	4 words
Line 5:	Synonym for the title	1 word

Look at the following word cinquain about war:

War

Leaving home

People dying daily

Can't stand the pain

Grief

Now try your own word cinquain on the feelings and emotions brought about from studying World War I. What types of words can help paint the picture you wish to create?

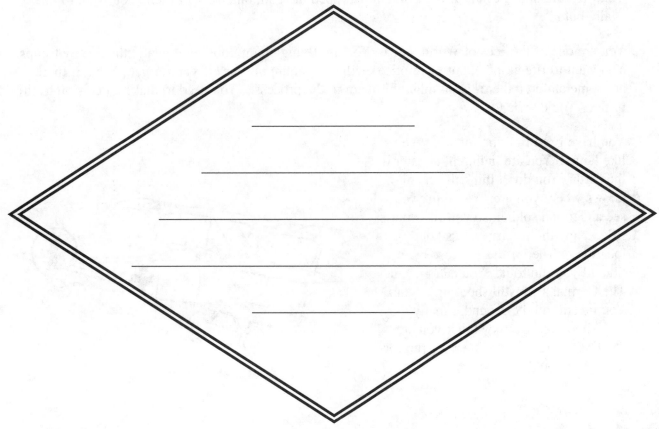

Finish the Story

Choose a paragraph to finish, and turn it into a short story of your imaginary war experience. Once you have finished, edit your short story. Be sure to look at capitalization, punctuation, and grammar. Submit a finished copy to your teacher to be displayed in your classroom.

1. All of your friends have volunteered to join the army. You don't want to join because you are scared. Everyone in town has been asking what you will do. You decide to . . .

2. You were injured last month in a battle. The doctor is coming to check on you in a few minutes. If you tell him that you feel fine, you will be sent back to fight. If you tell him that you are still in a great deal of pain, you can stay in the hospital. You have decided to tell the doctor that . . .

3. You are on front guard duty where your group is camped. You hear some noises that very well could be the enemy passing by. You know that you should investigate, but you don't want to get involved in something if you don't have to. You decide to . . .

4. You have been digging trenches all day. Your back is sore, your arms ache, and your clothes are drenched. The trench is damp and wet, and your shoes are filled with mud. Suddenly, the sergeant calls out that he needs a volunteer for sentry duty. You don't know what that is, but you are also sick of being in this trench. You choose to . . .

5. You are in the infantry. It is a dangerous job, but at least you don't have to go into battle first, like the field artillery. German machine gun bullets come thickly. You fire and your infantry begins to advance. You walk across No Man's Land and take the German trench. Most of the German soldiers are lying on the ground. One of them is standing with his gun pointed at you. You fire. He doesn't fall. It looks like he dropped his gun, but you can't tell. You want to fire again, but . . .

6. You are one of the aces of World War I. You are flying along, looking down at the enemy troops. You want to fire at them, but you notice civilians that are not far off your target. What if there are some children there? You might hit them in the process. You need to make a decision to fire or not. You decide to . . .

7. You have been fighting for what seems like hours. You are hiding in a crater in the earth. You don't think the enemy knows where you are. You think you see a German soldier, so you fire your rifle. Now the enemy knows your location. There is a tree close by. Should you run to it? You can't decide. The Germans are still shooting at you. You lie still on the ground. Finally they stop shooting. Do they think you are dead? Should you stay there or run for the tree? You decide to . . .

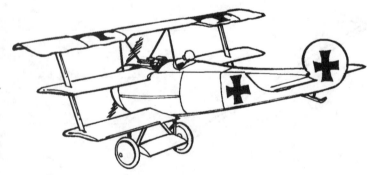

50

Newsworthy Notes

Select an event from World War I to report to the class. Use this form to jot down the basic information from your article. Then, on the back of this paper, write down your newspaper article. Be sure to reread your article to check for spelling, capitalization, and grammatical errors. Be prepared to discuss your article with the class.

Name of Article: _____

Date of Article: _____

Newspaper Source: _____

Get the basic facts from the newspaper article and place them under the correct category below:

What ? _____

_____

_____

When ? _____

_____

_____

Why ? _____

_____

_____

Where ? _____

_____

_____

How ? _____

_____

_____

Extension: Put together a class World War I newspaper. Choose appropriate articles for the front page and have students add art and drawings. Type the finished product on the computer and distribute!

Coordinating the Points

Most of the battles of World War I were fought in Europe. Using the coordinate points below, find some of the "hot spots" of World War I. The first one has been done for you.

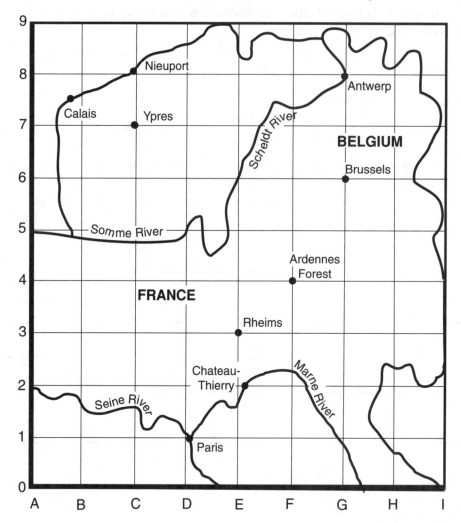

List the coordinate points for the following locations:

1. Ypres   <u> C–7 </u>

2. Chateau-Thierry   _____

3. Brussels   _____

4. Paris   _____

What locations can be found at the following coordinate points?

5. C–8_____

6. E–3_____

7. F–4_____

8. G–8_____

9. List the coordinate points for the Seine River:_____

Wars Are Hard to Predict

"You'll be home before the leaves have fallen from the trees." This famous quote from Kaiser Wilhelm II proved to be far from correct. Both sides thought it would be a short war, but war is filled with unexpected circumstances and problems. Using your best strategies, solve the following story problems.

1. The General called a meeting of lieutenants and sergeants to plan for the following day. Altogether, 178 lieutenants and sergeants attended the meeting, and there were 44 more sergeants than lieutenants. How many sergeants and how many lieutenants attended the meeting?

2. Soldiers Smith, Lutz, and Jones are at the supply tent together. Each of the soldiers has part of the list of things they need for their infantry. As they go to the checkout station, they each decide to get in a different line to save time. As Smith gets in line, he notices that there are three more people in front of him than are in front of Lutz, and there are two times as many people in front of Jones as there are in front of Lutz. The total number of people in front of Smith, Lutz, and Jones is 11. How many people are in front of each of the soldiers?

3. Captains Arthur and Floyd and First Lieutenants Short and Erickson are seated at a square table. Floyd is sitting to Short's left. Short is sitting across from a first lieutenant. Where is each soldier sitting at the table?

4. General Sharp is making his morning rounds around camp on his way to the mess tent. He goes north 3 tents, stops at Tent A and turns right. He goes east for 2 tents and then turns left and goes 1 tent north to the supply tent. Then he turns right, goes east 1 tent, and turns right again. He goes 4 tents south to the mess tent. When General Sharp leaves the mess tent, what is the quickest way for him to get back to where he began?

World War I Math Problems

1. Soldiers formed a line around a war torn field. One side measured nine acres across while the width of the field was two acres. How large an area did they surround?

2. Lt. Smith was ordered to build a trench that measured ten feet in length by six feet in width and five feet deep. How much room would there be inside the trench?

3. Company Eighteen received fire from the enemy. Captain Scott ordered them to return to their trenches as quickly as possible. They must crawl four feet north, then six feet around a wall, five feet toward a tree, and eleven feet across to reach a trench. What was the total number of feet they crawled?

4. "No man's land" was the desolate and dangerous land between the two fighting armies. At one point, no man's land measured 20 acres by 3 acres. What is its area?

5. Ammunition comes in square crates. Each side measured six feet. What was the volume of the crates?

Extra! Extra! Now write your own World War I story problem and have another student solve it. Check his or her answer to make sure that it was done correctly.

_____

_____

_____

_____

_____

The Deadly Virus

At the end of World War I in 1918, a worldwide influenza epidemic occurred in Europe, affecting millions of people. The influenza virus then spread throughout the continents and killed up to 20 million people, directly or indirectly through complications, in one year. In *World War I*, we read that the disease spread through the crowded camps of doughboys waiting to return home after the war. Some of the last doughboys to arrive in France were already infected. At one camp, men died at a rate of 250 per day.

Besides influenza, viruses cause measles, mumps, chicken pox, anthrax, yellow fever, and the common cold. Once a virus gets into your body, it searches for a cell to invade. A virus does not eat or grow, but it can reproduce. When it gets inside an organism, a virus begins to act like a living thing. It gets inside a cell and duplicates itself by the hundreds. These copies can then adjust themselves to a new environment, which makes it very hard to kill a virus. Look at the diagram below to understand how a virus works.

1. A virus passes through the cell wall. The virus loses its outer coating and releases nucleic acid.

2. Nucleic acid directs the cell to make more viruses. The virus is now releasing toxin into the blood stream.

3. The body then produces antibodies to fight the virus.

  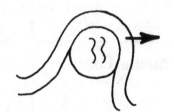

We are better able to handle these sicknesses today, but a virus can still cause lots of damage. One way that we can keep ourselves more healthy is by washing our hands. Why is washing our hands so important? Our hands touch everything and can therefore spread germs and disease. Try the experiment below:

Materials:

- 2 potato slices for each student
- 2 plastic zip top bags for each student
- hot water
- saucepan to blanch potatoes
- stovetop

Note to teacher: You can blanch the potatoes ahead of time.

Directions:

Peel a potato and boil it in hot water for approximately one minute. Slice the potato and set the slices aside to cool. When the potato slices have cooled, rub your fingers on a slice after you've been outside touching a lot of things. Then wash your hands with soap and water and dry your hands. Rub your fingers on the other potato slice. Put each slice in a separate plastic bag. Seal the bags. Leave the bags alone for a few days. How do the potatoes compare? After a few days have gone by, record your observations of both of the potatoes. What are your conclusions?

Deadly Gases

For the first time in the history of war, deadly gases were used by the Germans to fight the Allied troops. Various types of gases were used and experimented with on the Allied soldiers. On April 22, 1915, Germans released a greenish-yellow vapor on the Allied trenches. British troops were amazed as they had never seen such a sight before. Little did they know the deadly result and unimaginable pain of the gas. Germans used deadly chlorine gas, mustard gas, phosgene gas, and vomiting gases.

Investigate information on the gases used during World War I and the effects on the human body.

What	When	Why	How
chlorine gas			
mustard gas			
phosgene gas			
vomiting gas			

Extension:

Discuss the use of chemical warfare. Some say that this should never have been introduced to the war arsenal. Others feel that use of chemical warfare is justified. What do you think?

Famous Faces of WWI

Match the names of the following people with their involvement in World War I. You may use your book, *World War I*, and any other resource materials to help you.

A. He wrote the words to a famous World War I song.

_____ Archduke Francis Ferdinand

B. His assassination initiated the beginning of World War I.

_____ Woodrow Wilson

C. He wore a black moustache, stood straight and rigid, and had been the bold leader of Germany since 1890.

_____ General Ferdinand Foch

D. He urged the passing of the League of Nations and wrote the famous Fourteen Points.

_____ Captain Eddie Rickenbacker

_____ Lt. Colonel Wise

E. He was chosen to be the commander in chief of the American Expeditionary Force.

_____ George M. Cohan

F. He was the commander in chief of the French Army.

G. He was named the Supreme Allied Commander.

_____ Hans Otto Bischoff

H. He was the commander of the British Fifth Army.

_____ Kaiser Wilhelm

I. He directed the German defense at Belleau Wood.

_____ General John "Black Jack" Pershing

J. His battalion had stopped the Germans at their closest point to Paris.

_____ General Sir Hubert Gough

K. He was America's leading ace of World War I.

_____ General Henri Petain

Events of the Great War

Listed below are events that occurred during World War I. Place each event in the correct spot in the time line provided.

- President Wilson revealed his "Fourteen Points."
- First Armistice Day
- Belgium was invaded by Germany.

- United States declared war on Germany.
- Germans first used chlorine gas.
- British first used army tanks.

June 28, 1914	Archduke Francis Ferdinand was assassinated.
August 3, 1914	_____.
October 30, 1914	Turkey joined the Central Powers.
April 22, 1915	_____.
May 7, 1915	German submarine sank the *Lusitania*.
September 15, 1916	_____.
December 5, 1916	The Allies finally stop the Germans in the Battle of Verdun.
April 6, 1917	_____.
November 7, 1917	The Bolsheviks took over Russia.
January 8, 1918	_____.
September 26, 1918	Allies began their last attack on the Western Front.
November 11, 1918	_____.

Extension:

On Armistice Day, the German army surrendered to the Allies. Armistice today is now called Veterans Day, and it is a time set aside to honor war veterans. Research this day and contact your local veterans groups for more information.

Now and Then

Using the resources provided by your teacher or found in the library, do a comparison between the way things were during World War I and today. What things are similar? What things have changed?

	During World War I	**Today**
Transportation		
Food		
Clothing		
Health		
Education		
Recreation		
Arts		
Communication		

Extension:

How do you think things will be in the future? Write your answer on the back of this sheet.

Alliances

We form groups or alliances for all sorts of reasons. The Allies during World War I formed a group to fight together against the Central Powers. Sometimes alliances can bring about positive results, and sometimes negative results. Think about alliances of which you are a part. Perhaps you belong to a basketball team, a debate team, a group of friends, a chess team, a religious group, a family, etc. With these alliances in mind, write the answers to the questions on this page.

1. What is the definition of the word "alliance"? _____

   _____

   _____

2. Think of an alliance of which you are a part. _____

   _____

   _____

3. What is this alliance called? _____

   _____

   _____

4. How was this alliance formed? _____

   _____

   _____

5. What does this alliance do? Why? _____

   _____

   _____

6. Are these things positive or negative? _____

   _____

   _____

7. Why does being a member of this alliance make it easier to accomplish the desired results instead of doing it alone? _____

   _____

   _____

Trouble in the Cafeteria

(A skit to use in teaching about World War I)

Characters:		Students Assigned:
Narrator		_____
Steven	(Serbia)	_____
Rudy	(Russia)	_____
Frances	(France)	_____
Grace	(Great Britain)	_____
Geoff	(Germany)	_____
Aubrey	(Austria-Hungary)	_____

Narrator: The setting of our play is the cafeteria at lunch time. The cafeteria has been crowded this year and sometimes students must get there quickly to get a good seat. The back table is considered the best table because it is the furthest table from the teacher's table. Geoff and Aubrey have been friends for awhile and they usually sit at the back table. They are pretty cool sixth graders and tend to bully other students. They always have the latest clothes to wear and work out and are in good shape.

In the meantime, Rudy, Grace, and Frances have been friends for a long time and usually eat together at lunch break. Steven has recently become friends with Frances, and so the four have been eating together. Sometimes Grace will eat with Frances, Rudy, and Steven when she is not with other friends.

It just so happens that Frances does not like Geoff at all. They have had some arguments in the past and Geoff has really shown Frances who is boss. So you know what that means—Rudy and Grace don't like Geoff because of their friend Frances.

One day in the cafeteria, Steven decided that he wanted to sit at the table in the back. But Geoff and Aubrey always sit at the back table and really don't like Steven or any of his friends. Besides, everyone knows that the back table is off limits.

Steven: Come on, guys, let's go eat at the back table.

Rudy: Steven, you know that we can't eat there!

Steven: Who says we can't? Aubrey and Geoff? Who are they to tell us what to do? I am tired of sitting in the front. They aren't in charge of us.

Frances: Steven, I don't think we should. We could get into some trouble.

Narrator: But it was too late. Steven was already on his way to sit at the back table where Geoff and Aubrey were.

Steven: Hey! Scoot over and make some room. I've got some friends who are here to eat.

Trouble in the Cafeteria *(cont.)*

Aubrey: You can't just come and take over our table! Get out of here, wise guy!

Narrator: As you can guess, because Aubrey was bigger and stronger than Steven, Steven went ahead and sat with the group at the table near the front. Steven was upset by this and spent the rest of the lunch hour complaining about Aubrey and Geoff. Rudy, Frances, and Grace all agreed, but didn't say much. After lunch, everyone headed out to the basketball courts.

Steven: Hey, guys, I got a court. Come on and let's play a game of hoops.

Narrator: Steven, Rudy, and Frances played a game of half-court basketball for a while. Grace decided to play with them, and they played two on two. On the other half of the court were Geoff and Aubrey. Then Steven got another one of his brilliant ideas.

Steven: You know, it is too crowded to play two on two with only half a court. I think we should kick those guys at the other end off the court. Will you back me up if trouble starts?

Frances: But what about Geoff and Aubrey? They're kind of tough.

Steven: No sweat.

Narrator: Before Rudy, Frances, or Grace could say anything, Steven was strutting towards the other half of the court.

Frances: Steven is a pretty cool friend, but sometimes he gets kind of pushy.

Grace: I think he is going to get us all into trouble.

Rudy: I wish he wouldn't do this. Maybe we should stop him.

Frances: Oh, let him go. It will be okay.

Narrator: Rudy was more concerned than she was letting the others see. She did not think that it was right for Steven to be pushing Geoff and his friends around. But she liked being friends with Frances, so she didn't say anything.

Steven: Hey, Aubrey! We need more room to play our game, and since we were here first, I think you should let us have the whole court.

Trouble in the Cafeteria *(cont.)*

Aubrey: You were not here first! We were!

Steven: Were not!

Aubrey: Look, Steven, stop being a pain and let us play our game. You have half of a court just like we do. Besides, you're lucky we aren't taking the whole court!

Geoff: Besides, you don't want me to mess with you and your little friends, do you?

Narrator: Now Geoff was kind of a big guy, and so Steven decided that he better not push things any further—for the moment. He stomped back over to his side of the court.

Steven: I decided to be nice and let them keep that half of the court. We have enough room, I guess.

Frances: Do you want to play Around-the-World for a while?

Grace: Yeah, that sounds like fun! I get to start.

Rudy: I'm second.

Narrator: They played their game and were having a good time. It was Steven's turn to make the shot. He decided to shoot from the half court line. The other three waited near the basket to catch the ball. While Steven was in back, Aubrey's ball came rolling towards him. Steven bent down and picked up the ball. He got a funny look in his eyes.

Steven: Here's your ball!

Narrator: And with that, Steven chucked Aubrey's basketball over the fence and into the street.

Rudy: (under her breath) Oh no!

Aubrey: What did you do that for?! You . . . ! You . . . !

Narrator: Aubrey ran after her ball. When she got back, she was angrier than when she left. With that, Aubrey blew her top. She ran at Steven and tried to push him down, but Steven didn't budge. Then he pushed Aubrey—pretty hard, too. She fell backwards and nearly hit her head on the court. Geoff became furious and stomped over to Steven.

Geoff: Steven! It isn't polite to push people around. I'm going to slug you for that!

Steven: But she pushed me first!

Trouble in the Cafeteria *(cont.)*

Geoff: That's because you threw her basketball!

Narrator: Keep in mind that Geoff was a bigger dude than Steven and did not have any difficulty getting in a few good punches. Well, when Frances saw all this happening to his friend Steven, he felt like he should stick up for his friend. He came running to Steven's aid.

Frances: Look, Geoff, it's all a big misunderstanding. Let Steven go. You know how he is.

Geoff: No! He hit my friend and he is going to have to pay for it. And if you don't watch it, I'm going to have to teach you a little lesson too.

Narrator: Soon, everybody was involved in the fight on the basketball court. Rudy and Grace came to help because their friend Frances was getting beaten up by Geoff. Aubrey and a few other friends came along to help Geoff out.

You probably can figure out the rest of this story. Everybody involved got into big trouble! They all had detention for the rest of the month! You see how it can be with friendship? Sometimes we get into trouble just by the friendships we keep.

Teacher/Student Discussion:

Have you ever done something just because your friends did it? What was the result? When is it best to go along with the group? To stand alone? Discuss how the individual choices of the characters in the skit made an impact on someone else. Then, relate the skit to what happened during World War I.

War Bond Poster

Once the United States committed to fighting in World War I, it had the task of building a country that could prepare its army for war overseas. As President Wilson stated, "It is not an army we must shape and train for war, it is a nation." To bring in revenue, taxes were created on income, alcohol, tobacco, and other goods and services.

Funds were also borrowed from the American people through the sale of war bonds. War bonds were advertised through the help of well-known movie figures such as Charlie Chaplin and Mary Pickford, who made public appearances and appeared on war bond posters. Design your own war bond poster below to encourage American citizens to enlist in the war effort and to purchase war bonds.

Dilemma—A Time for Making Decisions

The decision to initiate or to become involved in war is difficult. War is used to solve problems, but war also brings misery and pain. Many lives are on the line and often unexpected results occur.

In everyday life, we also make difficult and tricky decisions when we attempt to solve problems. Choose a problem that is going on with you and another person, or a problem that is going on in the classroom or in the community. Identifying the problem is the first step. Next, one needs to look at all of the options to solve the problem. Using the diagram below, work through this problem to come to the best possible solution.

Solutions to a Problem

Problem Box

What is the problem? _____

Why is it a problem?_____

Who has the problem? _____

Solution Box

Solutions	Results
_____	_____
_____	_____
_____	_____

Desired Result Box

Why was this result chosen?_____

_____

_____

_____

_____

_____

Cooking on the Western Front

The food soldiers ate was generally of poor quality. But after a long day of battle, a common dinner on the Western Front was hard tack, or army biscuits, and creamed beef. Using the recipes below, see if you can cook up this filling meal.

Hard Tack

Ingredients

$^1/_3$ cup (85 mL) shortening

1 $^3/_4$ cups (590 mL) all-purpose flour

2 $^1/_2$ tsp. (12.5 mL) baking powder

$^3/_4$ tsp. (3 mL) salt

$^3/_4$ cup (180 L) milk

Directions

Heat oven to 450° F (230° c). Cut shortening into flour, baking powder and salt with fork until mixture looks like fine crumbs. Stir in just enough milk so that dough leaves sides of bowl and forms a ball. (Too much milk makes dough sticky, not enough makes biscuits dry.) Do not stir too much, as this will make the biscuits tough.

Place dough onto lightly-floured surface. Knead lightly 10 times. Roll $^1/_2$-inch thick. Cut with floured 2-inch biscuit cutter or and slice into squares. Place on clean cookie sheet about 1 inch apart. Bake until golden brown, 10 to 12 minutes. Immediately remove from cookie sheet. Makes about 1 dozen biscuits.

Creamed Beef

Most soldiers ate corned beef rather than hamburger, but the following recipe comes close to the real thing.

Ingredients

• 1 lb. (453.6 g) hamburger   • 2 tbsp. (30 mL) flour   • 1 cup (240 mL) milk

Directions

Fry hamburger in skillet on medium heat until it is well done. Do not remove the grease. Add the flour to the meat while it is still on the heat. Once the flour is mixed in well with the meat, slowly add the milk. Continue to cook on medium heat until all flour is dissolved, creating a smooth gravy. Remove from heat and serve over hard biscuits. Serves four.

World War I Quiz Game

Preparation:

On a separate piece of paper, write the names of the four WWI Quiz categories: WWI Battles, Central Powers, Allies, and United States Involvement. (You may also create your own categories based on information taught in your classroom.) Then, on separate index cards, write down four questions for each category on one side of the card. Some suggested questions are listed below:

WWI Battles

Which battle was fought in an old one-square-mile hunting preserve? *(Belleau Wood)*

What strategy was commonly used as a form of "natural" protection by individual soldiers to fight during World War I? *(trenches)*

What was the name that World War I was first known by? *(the Great War)*

In what battle did the Allies halt the German drive? *(Battle of Verdun)*

Central Powers

Name the main countries that formed the Central Powers. *(Germany, Austria-Hungary, Turkey, and Bulgaria)*

Name two leaders from the Central Powers. *(Hans Otto Bischoff from Germany, Kaiser Wilhelm II from Germany)*

When did Germany finally sign an armistice with the Allies? *(November 11, 1918)*

What did the Germans use for the first time in the history of warfare? *(deadly chlorine gas)*

Allies

Name the main countries that formed the Allies. *(Great Britain, France, Russia, and United States)*

Name two leaders from the Allies. *(General Pershing from U.S., General Petain from France)*

When did the United States finally join the Allies? *(April 6, 1917)*

What did the British army first use in September of 1916? *(army tanks)*

United States Involvement

Who was president when the United States entered World War I? *(President Woodrow Wilson)*

Name two famous people involved in WWI from the United States. *(Lt. Colonel Wise, General Pershing)*

How was the United States involved when the *Lusitania* was sunk? *(124 passengers were from the Many people felt that the U.S. should become involved with the war at this time.)*

What did the U.S. Senate not ratify at the end of the war? *(The Treaty of Versailles)*

World War I Quiz Game *(cont.)*

On the reverse side of the index card, write the numbers 5, 10, 15, and 20. These numbers will be used to tabulate points later in the game. Place these cards question side down under each category so that the points are showing. (See diagram below.)

Earned points	WWI Battles	Central Power	Allies	U.S. Involvment
Team 1	20	20	20	20
Team 2	15	15	15	15
Team 3	10	10	10	10
Team 4	5	5	5	5

Directions: Divide the class into four or five teams. Each team chooses a spokesperson for their team and a team name. Decide which team will go first. Each team chooses a category and card to try to win. The monitor (teacher) reads the question and the team has 30 seconds to discuss the answer to the question. The spokesperson for the team states the answer. If the answer is correct, the team receives the points on the index card and continues their turn with another index card. Have the teams keep their scored index cards on the scoreboard so at the end of the game the points can be tabulated. If the answer is incorrect, the card is placed back on the chalkboard under its category and the next team in order receives a turn. Play continues in this fashion until all the index cards have been chosen and answered. The team with the most points at the end of the game wins.

Tic-Tac-Go

Using questions from the books, student pages, and any other resources, your class can play Tic-Tac-Go as a review of the thematic material on World War I.

Directions:

1. On the chalkboard, draw the familiar tic-tac-toe grid.

2. Divide the class in half. One team will be the X's and one team will be the O's.

3. The teacher determines which group will go first, the X's or the O's. The teacher then selects a question and poses it to the competing team of X's or O's.

4. The competing team chooses a team member to answer the question.

5. The team member responds with the correct or incorrect answer.

6. The competing team either agrees or disagrees with the response.

7. If the competing team answers correctly, they get to place an "X" or an "O" in the tic-tac-toe grid.

8. The other competing team now selects a team member to answer the question and the procedure continues.

9. The winning team is determined by the first team to place its "X" or "O" in three adjoining squares vertically, horizontally, or diagonally.

10. Continue until all students have had the opportunity to participate.

World War I Projects

As a culminating activity, choose a project from the list below that you would like to share with another class in your school. A written description of your plan should be completed and signed by the teacher. (See page 72 for "WWI Project Contract.")

- Make a poster-sized map of the world showing all the countries involved in World War I. Include an easy-to-read key identifying the Allies and the Central Powers. Place dates, names, and other important information on your map as well. Be prepared to share this in front of the class discussing the role each country played in WWI.

- Research the sinking of the *Lusitania* and write a newspaper article as if you were a newspaper reporter at the time assigned to cover this event. Remember to answer the five questions: what, when, where, why, and how.

- Research the League of Nations and the Treaty of Versailles. What role did the League of Nations play and what was the result at the end of World War I? Compare and contrast the League of Nations with the United Nations.

- Design a picture book of the different uniforms and the new weapons used in World War I. Be prepared to discuss the importance of uniforms in a war and what each uniform represents.

- Write an historical fiction story about what life would be like during World War I. Each chapter in the book could be about a character from a different country involved in World War I. Be sure to research to assure accurate information.

- Create a time line of World War I with small illustrations and brief summaries of events at each significant point in history. This should be done on poster board so that it is big enough to read. Have a brief discussion about the changes that occurred as a result of each event.

- Prepare a report on how the war changed the lives of women. Provide examples of the different types of jobs that women did. Did women doing "men's work" receive the same pay as the men? Compare the types of jobs at that time with the jobs that women do today. Compare the hours spent at work as well.

World War I Projects *(cont.)*

- Research one of the major battles or invasions of World War I. Be sure to describe the scenery and the country where the battle took place. What was the result of the battle? Describe its strategy and significance in an oral report that lasts approximately five minutes.

- If at all possible, interview a veteran of World War I. Prepare a list of questions ahead of time and tape the interview so that you can listen to the responses again later. Be sure to ask questions about the veteran's family and what their feelings were about the situation. If possible, you may even invite this veteran to come to the class to answer more questions. Be sensitive to the fact that this is a subject that may be difficult to discuss and your questions need to be considerate of that.

- Pretend it is the year 1917. Imagine that you are the President of the United States. What would you say to the country? Prepare a speech that will be heard all over the United States and present it as an oral presentation to the class. Be sure to dress up as a president would.

- Learn some songs that were popular during this time period. Go to your public library to check out recordings of these songs. You could lead a sing-a-long and teach students some new songs or dances that were popular during this time. A short discussion on the meaning of the words in the songs could also be done.

World War I Project Contract

Student Name_____

The project that I have chosen to complete is _____.

Due date_____

What do I need to do to complete this project?_____

_____

What will the finished product look like? _____

_____

How will I share my finished project?_____

_____

Other things that I need to remember while I am working on my project:_____

_____

_____

Student Signature

_____

Teacher Signature

Bulletin Board and Center Ideas

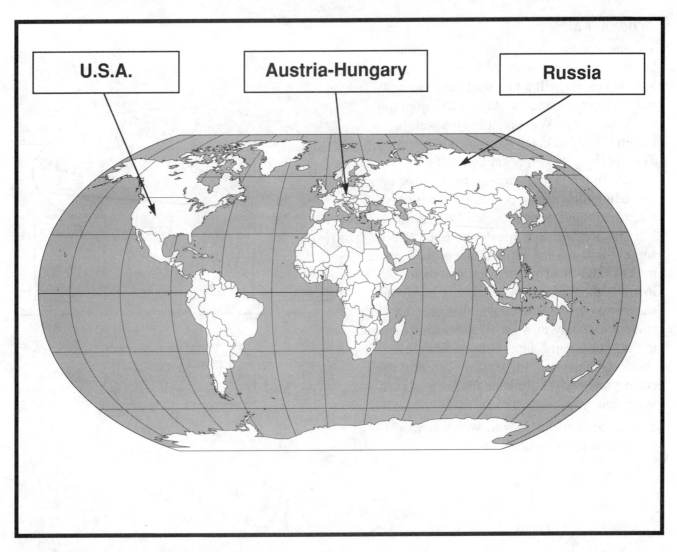

World War I: A Time of Change

Put up a map of the world. Use string or yarn to connect easily read labels to the countries involved in World War I. Have students research each country's position in the war, writing a one-page summary to post.

World War I: The War to End All Wars

Mount illustrations of World War I scenes on colored construction paper. Post student written historical fiction stories of this time period written by students.

Mention My Invention and Bright Ideas!

When students have designed their inventions and have pictures drawn (page 24), hang their drawings on this bulletin board. As a border for this bulletin board, cut out and post pictures of different inventions.

Bulletin Board and Center Ideas *(cont.)*

True or False

To reinforce the concepts and information being taught in the study of World War I, this learning center will allow students to identify true or false statements. Mount a map of the world or a large WWI picture on a wall or bulletin board to catch the students' attention. Then place a "true" pocket and a "false" pocket up next to the large picture or map. On a desk or small table, place a box covered with construction paper and labeled "statements." Fill this box with statements about the WWI, some true and some false. Students will come to the center, read a statement, and then place it in either the true or false pocket. Change the statements daily. You could even assign a student each day to write 10 statements to go in the "statements" box. Students can self-check their work at this learning center if the correct answer is written on the back of each statement strip.

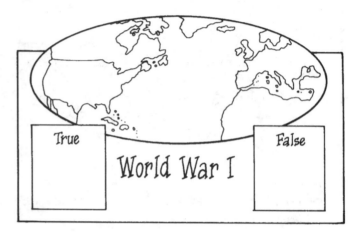

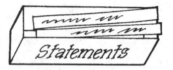

This same idea can be done with statements that are either facts or opinions.

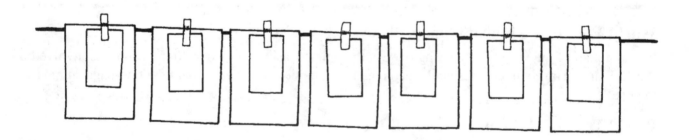

World War I Time Line

Hang a piece of string all the way around the room. Place a piece of paper around the string for each year of World War I. Start at one end of the room and as each event of World War I is discussed, have students hang an index card with a paper clip or clothespin on the correct spot on the time line. Students can use this time line as a reference.

Did You Know?

Each day, place a different fact about World War I from the list below on a specifically designated bulletin board. These facts will spur interest and questions as the students learn more about World War I.

- In 1914 all the khaki dye for the uniforms of the British army was manufactured in Germany.

- In 1900 Britain produced more coal than France, Germany, Russia, Austria-Hungary, and Italy combined.

- The American soldiers were dubbed 'doughboys.'

- Nick Muhall was the first American soldier to be captured.

- AEF stood for the American Expeditionary Force.

- Germans were the first to use chlorine gas. They also used mustard gas and vomiting gas.

- Some U.S. recruits were from such remote areas that they did not know their birth dates and last names. The army assigned these men last names and birth dates.

- Of the 129 children aboard the *Lusitania*, 94 died.

- Each doughboy carried 200 rounds of ammunition, six boxes of hardtack, two cans of corned beef, and a one-quart canteen into the battle of the Argonne.

- Major Charles Wittlesey used homing pigeons to let the American troops know of their whereabouts. One such homing pigeon, "Cher Ami," was nearly shot to death but kept flying until it reached its destination.

- Many U.S. soldiers died not of battle wounds, but of disease and exposure to the elements.

- Seven hundred men who returned from the war had hands or feet amputated.

- Within minutes of the cease fire, American and German troops were exchanging cigarettes, food rations, soap, belt buckles, and even some German army medals.

- The one-square-mile Belleau Wood was an old hunting preserve and was half of the size of Central Park in New York City.

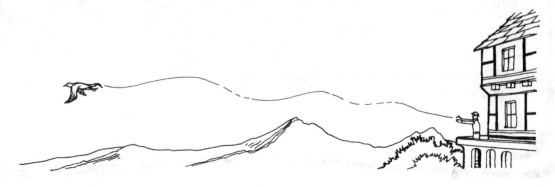

Parent Letter

_____

(Date)

Dear Parents,

Your child is about to embark on a study of World War I. Few events in history had such a lasting and traumatic effect as did the first world war. Learning about this war can help teach the future generation about decisions and consequences. Some of the issues and themes of this unit include sacrifice, loss of life, conflict, resolution, alliance, survival, war, politics, etc. We encourage you to discuss these issues with your child. Review and read the materials your child brings home.

This unit will feature two highly acclaimed books *After the Dancing Days* by Magaret I. Rostkowski, and *World War I* by Peter Bosco to help students understand and learn about the effects and events of World War I. We invite you to read these books as well.

This unit will also include a wide variety of lessons and activities in the areas of language arts, math, science, art, drama, life skills, and social studies.

We have set up a World War I Research Center that has been filled with books, resources, and other materials to aid in our study. We would like to enlist your help and support in our efforts. We are looking for guest speakers, books, resources, and additional materials you have available. You may also have World War I memorabilia at home such as medals, life stories, newspaper clippings, letters, photographs, etc., that you might be willing to share with the class. Please contact me if you have any information or materials that would be beneficial in our study.

We appreciate your help in making this study of World War I a success. We look forward to learning as much as we can about this time in history.

Sincerely,

_____

(Teacher)